*N*othing
to Be Ashamed Of

*N*othing
to Be Ashamed Of:

Growing Up with Mental Illness in Your Family

Sherry H. Dinner, Ph.D.

Lothrop, Lee & Shepard Books
New York

First Edition 1 2 3 4 5 6 7 8 9 10

Library of Congress Cataloging in Publication Data
Dinner, Sherry H. Nothing to be ashamed of.
Bibliography: p.   Includes index. 1. Mentally ill—Family relationships—
Juvenile literature. 2. Mental illness—Juvenile literature. I. Title.
RC460.2.D56 1989 616.89 88-13244
ISBN 0-688-08482-6 (lib. bdg.) ISBN 0-688-08493-1 (pbk.)

To my patients, who inspired me
To my family, who gave me encouragement
To A.S., who took me seriously

ACKNOWLEDGMENTS

I am grateful to the following individuals who were kind enough to take time from their busy schedules to review and comment on specific chapters of my book: Catherine Morrison, L.I.S.W., Candida Sicre, M.D., Elena Wolfenson, M.D., Joseph Kahl, M.D., Donald Kellon, M.D., and Leo Romisher, O.D., all of Ohio Permanente Medical Group; Meir Gross, M.D., Windsor Hospital; and John P. Wilson, Ph.D., Cleveland State University.

Ginny Steiner did her usual excellent job in typing the manuscript.

Dorothy Briley, Editor-in-Chief, and Dinah Stevenson, Executive Editor, Lothrop, Lee & Shepard Books, patiently guided me through my first publishing experience and gave many helpful suggestions.

Contents

CONTENTS

Nothing
to Be Ashamed Of

Introduction

This book is for young people who are growing up with a mentally ill family member. It could be a parent, a brother or sister, or even a grandparent that you're close to. The fact that one of your relatives is mentally ill has most likely been making your life complicated. What I'd like to do is explain what makes mental illness so hard on family members, and how this book can help you.

Try to imagine for a moment what it would be like if you and your family suddenly moved to a country where people spoke a different language and followed different rules. The people there might eat certain foods with their fingers that we eat with a knife and fork. Or they might eat things that we don't think of as food, such as grasshoppers! If you went to a movie there after learning the language, you might find that people laughed at things that didn't seem at all funny to you. If the people had a suspicious attitude toward strangers, you might feel sad and confused when you tried unsuccessfully to make friends. If you tried to figure out why the people acted this way, your "American" explanations would probably be wrong.

One way to describe the actions of mentally ill people is to say that such people are following different rules. These rules might be a result of differences in the way their brains work or faulty ideas they've learned during their lives. If you don't know about mental illness, you are likely to have the same kinds of confusion, sadness, and other reactions in dealing with a mentally ill person that you would if you moved to a foreign country. You might think your mentally ill family member was purposely trying to embarrass, annoy, or hurt you. You might start to stay away from the ill person whenever you could. By learning about mental illness, you can help both yourself and your ill relative.

As boys and girls get to be ten or twelve, many things in their lives join together to make them worry a lot about themselves. Bodies are changing in preparation for adulthood, creating those ugly pimples and worrisome body odor. Concerns about whether you are developing too fast or too slowly in comparison with your friends can make you feel

2

strange or embarrassed. Your whole ability to think is becoming more advanced, allowing you to think about the past, present, and future in ways you never could before. With all these changes to worry about and adjust to, it's no wonder that young people often ask themselves, "Am I normal?" With a mentally ill person in the family, it's an easy step, then, to the thought, "Am I getting to be like _____?" Reading about the most common types of mental illness and what they really involve can help you to put your normal worries into perspective.

This book can help by giving you specific techniques and ideas on how to deal with the problems created by living with a mentally ill person. What's more, you can feel a great sense of relief, hope, and encouragement knowing that others have been through similar difficulties and lived to tell about it. One of the worst things about the shame and secrecy surrounding mental illness is that those who are trying to cope with an ill family member have been left on their own. By reading about others like yourself, you can find that it's possible to have a good life.

In the rest of this book, I will describe the most common types of serious mental illness and what we have learned about them. I'll talk about the different helping professionals you will probably meet in the course of your relative's treatment, and how they might be able to help you. I will discuss the kinds of treatments used for different problems, and I will tell how family members can help one another and themselves.

One thing I won't be talking about is alcoholism, even though some mentally ill people use alcohol or drugs. This can be their way to quiet the voices they hear or calm the intense excitement or nervousness they feel. In these cases, the alcohol or drug use is not the main problem but a result of the mental illness.

Many books have been written and support groups have been started for the families and children of alcoholics and drug abusers in the last ten years. Unfortunately, there is less help and attention for families of the mentally ill at this point. Therefore, I have concentrated on mental illness.

In order that the privacy of the families I have worked with can be protected, the examples throughout this book are fictional. Each one combines research findings and typical experiences of mental illness with features (in disguised form) of real people, to help you understand what happens in a particular disorder.

1

◆

What Is Mental Illness?

In order for you to understand exactly what kinds of problems I will be discussing in this book, try thinking about something that we usually take for granted. All of us depend, in many ways, on people around us having the same general ideas about what is real. The sky is blue, the grass is green, and if today is Friday, tomorrow will be Saturday. We don't even think of talking about these things because everyone agrees on them. If someone tried to argue with us about these facts, what would we call that person? "Crazy."

Mentally ill people often find themselves alone in believing that certain things are real or that certain ideas are true. They may believe that they are on the verge of a major discovery when they really are not. They may think that they are fat when in fact they are thin. You can imagine the kinds of problems this can create for them. They can become very quiet and private, afraid to say what they think because others will disagree or laugh, something that seems to happen a lot. They are hurt very easily when people disagree with them, until their anger builds into rage. This in turn makes their families or friends feel that they have to be careful about what they say. The family members and friends might even decide that it's just easier to avoid these people. School and jobs are difficult for such people to handle, and those in charge of the schools or jobs might tell them to stay away because they don't "fit in." The mentally ill frequently find themselves alone more and more, having to rely on their own, probably wrong, explanations of why people avoid them. Much of the suffering mental illness brings stems from the affected person's different way of seeing reality.

The Problems of Mental Illness

Two case histories can show how problems develop as a result of mental illness. Mary had trouble making friends from the time she was in junior high. She was afraid that if people really knew her, they would disappoint her in some way. They might "blab" her secrets around school, or find out what she knew in her subjects and use it to get better grades themselves.

In high school Mary kept mainly to herself, but she spent hours envying the popular girls. She felt happy imagining how she might get to be someone whom everyone else would envy. Gradually the gap between how the kids saw her and what she imagined herself to be became wider and wider. Her classmates saw her as a "weirdo" who whispered and smiled to herself and kept her books clutched tightly to her chest. In Mary's mind, she was just about to discover a new substance that would end all air or water pollution, making her famous.

At home, whatever her parents said to try to change her ideas made no dent in her thinking. As a result her father became upset, to the point of screaming at her. His screaming, in turn, upset Mary, making her feel that he was against her.

Thinking that she was on the verge of a big discovery and that people would steal her ideas, Mary stayed away from other kids. They in turn avoided her or teased her. She felt that all the smiles and laughter of the boys and girls in her classes were aimed at her. Even when the others weren't around, Mary could hear them laughing. Because her "work," which was mostly nonsense, took up a lot of her time, she also wasn't able to learn much in school. This caused her teachers to become frustrated with her.

Mary had trouble seeing herself and other people as they really were. This led to poor relationships with her classmates, teachers, and family members. In addition, she couldn't achieve what she might have been able to if she weren't mentally ill.

A boy named Jon also had trouble seeing reality as other people do. When Jon was in high school, classmates knew him as a quiet type who studied a lot and got good grades but hardly ever spoke in class. When he came to school one day bubbling with excitement and talking almost nonstop, everyone knew something was wrong. Jon was also bursting with energy outside of school. He stayed up late taking household gadgets apart to make them work more efficiently. His parents became frustrated, as they tried to live a peaceful life with someone who slept only three hours a night. They had trouble convincing him to see a doctor, but finally he went.

Fortunately, Jon was able to get the treatment he needed. He was diagnosed as manic-depressive and put on medication. His treatment included having his blood tested routinely to make sure the medication was at the right level to work properly. He also had appointments with a psychologist, to help him deal with problems in a useful way.

Like Mary and her family, Jon and his family had to cope with many aspects of mental illness. Unless his condition was under control, his relationships with other people were disrupted. Many enjoyable areas of his life, such as school, friends, family, and sports, became a confused mess. He, too, was unable to do the things he was capable of. And, like Mary, he had an illness that was serious and would not go away by itself.

From reading about these two people, it's easy to see the seriousness of mental illness. People sometimes toss around words like "crazy" or "insane," but the person with a mental illness has specific defects in his thoughts, feelings, or behavior. Knowing what mental illness is can help when you feel that you are different or don't fit in, something everyone feels at times. Being clear about what mental illness is not, you won't mistake common and minor types of emotional upset for mental illness.

Normal Reactions to Change

Reaching a new stage of life often leads to temporary problems. That is partly because any big change in our lives forces us to find new ways to act, which can be uncomfortable. For example, some women feel "down" and weepy for a time after hav-

9

ing a baby. This postpartum depression, as it is called, usually goes away by itself or with some brief counseling, and is not mental illness. Adolescence is another stage when temporary emotional ups and downs can occur. For many young people, the teen years may be linked with strong feelings of self-doubt. Some teenagers may feel almost constant anger toward their parents for being so "out of it." Once this period of life is past, these feelings go away.

Besides these stages that people go through as they mature, events outside our control can occur at any time and create stress. For example, suppose your grandparent dies, or you have to move to a new school district or a different state. It's common to go through a period of grief, in the first example, or loneliness, in the second. Whether these feelings go away on their own after a while, or with the help of a psychologist or social worker, they are normal reactions to common stresses.

Minor Emotional Problems

Other disturbances in behavior or emotions are less common. These are serious enough that, without the attention of a mental health professional, they would continue to get worse. If they are treated, the problems can go away completely. For example, if every time you took a test, you started sweating and breathing hard and feeling pressure in your head and chest, you would probably be having test anxiety. At all other times, such as when you were with friends or participating in sports, you could be perfectly fine. If the test anxiety continued, it would become more and more difficult to treat. You might also begin to feel ashamed or worried about yourself, until even those areas of your life that weren't connected with test taking might start to suffer.

This would not be mental illness. Your ideas about yourself and other people would be based on reality. Most areas of your life would not be a problem for you, and you could succeed according to your ability, except where tests were concerned. Your relationships would continue as usual, and the anxiety could be treated successfully in a number of sessions with the school psychologist.

A person with low self-confidence might find it hard to speak up in disagreements with friends for fear of making them angry. Donna grew up in a family in which people weren't comfortable talking openly about disagreements. If her father did something that hurt her mother's feelings, her mother's response was to not talk to him for two days, then act as if nothing had happened. By the time Donna was in junior high, she found herself worrying about what her friends would do if she expressed a different opinion, so she kept her thoughts to herself. Her built-up feelings of anger and frustration began to come out in another way: overeating. In order to keep overeating from turning into a serious problem, she talked to a mental health professional and learned how to work out disagreements without the fear of losing friends. Like the test anxiety example, this was not mental illness. People outside the family had no idea that something was bothering Donna, and psychological help ended the problem.

Mental illness makes it hard for the person to have correct ideas about himself or herself and the world, and hurts the person's relationships with family and friends. It keeps the person from achieving what he or she is capable of doing, affects most areas of the person's life, and is usually long-lasting. In the next chapter, I'll talk about how family members often react to the difficult situations that arise because of mental illness. If you are living with someone who is mentally ill, chances are many of the examples will be familiar to you.

2

◆

Reactions to Living with a Mentally Ill Person

Although the experiences described in this chapter may not happen to every person or family, they are all common feelings and reactions. Seeing that other people have had these experiences can help you realize that it isn't strange or bad to have these feelings. Unfortunately, when someone in your family is mentally ill, you might have such a jumble of mixed-up reactions that it's hard to tell what you're feeling! It can be helpful just to start putting a label on your emotions.

Common Feelings

Perhaps you've had thoughts like these: "Will I have to look after my brother some day when Mom and Dad are no longer alive?" "What if my sister is living on the streets somewhere?" "How will I go to

13

college if Dad is spending all his money on Mom's treatment?" *Worry* is common when you're dealing with a type of illness that is unpredictable and long-term. It's hard to put aside these concerns because there are no sure or comforting answers to the questions. No one really knows how long treatment will take or how the person will respond to it.

More specific things that might happen at any time, rather than off in the future, give rise to *fears*. Living with a depressed person who has talked about wanting to die can make you afraid that one day the person may die by suicide. You may fear that the arguments your parents are having every day about how to deal with your brother will result in a divorce. Or you could be afraid that the shyness you feel when speaking in front of the class is a sign that you will become mentally ill, especially if your brother also used to be shy and later developed mental illness. Fears, too, are hard to put aside.

Overwhelming *sadness* may come when family members start to face the idea that their loved one will always have this illness. Knowing that there's no magic pill or operation to make the person healthy can lead some family members to mourn for their lost hopes of how things might have been.

It's not unusual for family members to be *angry*. They may think: "It's not fair that Dad has to spend

14

his life worrying about his next breakdown." "Why can't I have a normal family like everyone else?" "I never asked for a schizophrenic sister!" Or even, "I wish he would leave and never come back so I can go on with my life." One problem with anger is that it often gets kept inside. What is the point of telling someone who is mentally ill how angry you feel? However, when angry feelings are held in over a period of time, they usually find a way of coming out, as I'll explain later.

Many family members feel *guilty* at times. If you get good grades, then knowing that your ill brother might not even complete an English course can make you feel bad sometimes about your success, even though it isn't logical to feel this way. Young people who have had angry thoughts may feel guilty for even thinking these thoughts. "How can I be angry with her? It's not her fault. I must be a terrible person." This might happen when they lose patience with an elderly, confused grandparent.

There's also the shame and *embarrassment* that go with having a mentally ill family member. "If my friends knew my brother is crazy, they'd never want me to be around them." "How can I bring my boyfriend over if my mom is in one of her moods?" "I can't talk to my friends about my father—they'd never understand!"

15

Reactions to Symptoms of Mental Illness

Sometimes people's strongest reactions to having a mentally ill family member are caused by the symptoms of the illness. Cathy's dad served in the Vietnam War. She had seen his uniform and occasionally had heard him chatting on the phone with old friends from his platoon. But he never talked about what it was like in the army. The only clue she had that he still suffered from his memories of the war was the terrible nightmares he had once in a while. He would suddenly sit up in bed, screaming and shouting. Although he looked as if he were awake, he did not seem to hear or see Cathy and her mother when they tried to calm him down. The fact that Cathy never knew when these nightmares would happen made her nervous about going to sleep. She worried that tonight Dad might not snap out of it. Sometimes she stayed awake until one or two in the morning. Paying attention in her classes the next day wasn't easy.

Embarrassing, odd behavior and confused behavior of some mentally ill people can affect family members' daily lives. Other people with mental illness have symptoms that aren't so much annoying or embarrassing as they are scary. Violent behavior, especially, can be frightening to see. The fear then spills over into peaceful times, as you think, "When will it happen again?"

In your family, are there symptoms that have been particularly upsetting to you? Can you name the feelings that these symptoms have stirred up in you? Although it may seem easier to push the feelings aside, putting a name on them and thinking about how they're affecting you can be a lot more useful. This can even be the first step in finding ways to deal with what's bothering you.

What can make the symptoms of mental illness especially hard to put up with is knowing that they can often be prevented. Many medications have been shown to reduce or even eliminate some of these symptoms. Unfortunately, the mentally ill person may decide that he doesn't need the medicine. This may be because his thinking and reasoning abilities are disrupted by the illness. What others see as strange behavior seems to him normal. In other cases, the person may not like certain side effects of the medicine. And it sometimes happens that the person may actually miss his symptoms, if those symptoms made him feel full of energy and able to tackle any problem in the world. When Jon, who was manic-depressive, started to feel things were getting dull, he missed the way his symptoms had given him so much energy. Although Jon

17

managed to push aside the temptation to stop taking his medication, others are not able to do this. If your relative is acting strange and refuses to take a prescribed medication that would ease the symptoms, this can be especially frustrating for you.

Dealing with the Mental Health System

Disturbing behavior isn't the only aspect of mental illness that can cause distress for family members. Some families have found that their contacts with mental health professionals are at times more upsetting than helpful. For many years the accepted ideas about the cause of mental illness were focused on the ill person's early experiences. In particular, how the parents acted toward their growing child was thought to be the reason for any emotional problems that arose later on. This is no longer thought to be the only explanation. New ideas about the causes of mental illness are taking other factors into account. Even so, you may be asked questions that make you feel you are being accused of helping to cause the problems. Certainly no one can be a perfect parent, child, brother, or sister. When someone with a lot of diplomas on the wall asks about things that happened years ago, it's easy to feel that

18

your answers will prove whether you were a "good" or "bad" influence.

It can be especially discouraging and frustrating to talk with professionals during the early stages of the illness. Because most mental illnesses develop gradually, it's easy to think, at first, "It's just a stage she's going through." This is what Mary's parents believed when she wouldn't play with other children. As Mary got older and her behavior became more unusual and difficult to manage, they took her to a psychologist. Although Mary was having serious trouble participating in her classes and getting along with other kids, she wouldn't reveal her strange ideas to the doctor. Without some cooperation from her, the doctor was unable to find out what her problem really was.

It's understandable that doctors are not eager to put a label of mental illness on someone quickly. The fear and hopelessness that family members feel can cause doctors to speak cautiously, especially if the symptoms aren't clear-cut. Therefore, when the symptoms drag on or get worse, the family may feel disappointed, confused, or angry about not receiving a definite explanation. Since most people hate to think that their relative is mentally ill, they keep hoping that a quick cure to the problems will be found. When Mary's parents and sister were told, finally, that she had schizophrenia, they were sad and frightened. At the same time, they were relieved to know that there was an explanation for her behavior.

The symptoms of mental illness can be so strange and confusing that it's hard to understand, without help, why the ill person is behaving that way. However, even after a diagnosis was made, you may have found it hard to get information from the doctor about your relative's illness. If the doctor has said, "I'm not able to give you that information because patients have a right to confidentiality," this isn't unusual. He or she is not just trying to shut you out. Legally, a psychiatrist, psychologist, or social worker is not allowed to repeat what a patient has said without the patient's permission, except in very special situations. If you are trying to make sense out of your brother's keeping to his room most of the time, for example, it is upsetting and frustrating to feel that someone has the explanation but won't share it.

Because most mentally ill people need long periods of treatment and perhaps occasional hospitalizations, many families have money problems. They find that their health insurance covers only a part of the cost of treatment. If this is true in your family, it may mean that your mother or father will need a second job to afford the treatment. Naturally, this will mean less time spent with you and more chores for you around the house. You may feel sad or even guilty that the best treatment program available is too expensive for your family. You might even start to imagine, "If only we could afford Dr. So-and-so, everything would be fine," which is probably not true. Or you might feel angry at the doctor for charging so much. Perhaps your relative will need to switch from a private doctor with high fees to one at a state or county hospital with much lower costs. You might find yourself taking part in family therapy sessions with first one and then another doctor. Repeating your story with each new doctor or social worker, and feeling that you are starting all over, can be frustrating, especially if such changes seem to cause a setback in your ill relative's progress. Although treatment costs are your parents' responsibility and not yours, the worry and frustration of money problems may be hard for you to avoid.

Coping with Other Family Members

You may already be aware of the problems that can come from dealing with the other members of your family apart from the mentally ill person. Mark

21

was upset that his sister had dieted down to eighty-eight pounds, but he hated to see their father trying to force his sister to eat and gain weight. He realized that his sister would try to fool their father and that only a hospital or other treatment program would be effective. It also bothered him that his parents hardly noticed his grades from his second semester of college. They were so busy trying to help his sister that they couldn't take their minds off her problem.

Your parents or a sister or brother might give in to all the demands of the ill person, even if you think this isn't helpful. Or people outside your immediate family, such as cousins or aunts and uncles, might avoid talking about your ill family member. Mary's sister, Carla, felt hurt that their cousin never asked how Mary was doing. People often feel uncomfortable and unsure about what they should or shouldn't say about the ill person. When they deal with their discomfort by ignoring the situation, you may feel hurt and alone in your problems.

Putting It into Perspective

I've been focusing on the problems of living with someone who is mentally ill and the feelings that grow out of these difficulties. It's important to remember that this is just one part of your life. Other areas—school, friends, hobbies—are important, too. They can bring you good or bad feelings that have nothing to do with your relative's mental illness. In this respect, you're not too different from your friends.

You probably know other young people who have difficult situations in their lives, such as divorce, or the death of a family member, or serious physical illness. Perhaps you've even been aware of how they are dealing with these troubles. It's often easier to notice how other people are coping with problems than to realize how you are handling the challenges in your own life.

Choices in Dealing with Your Emotions

One of the most important things you can do is to recognize how you're reacting to your relative's illness and the problems that go along with it. This is important because the way you deal with these feelings can affect how your own life turns out later. Nobody likes the unpleasant feelings I've talked about, so people sometimes make serious mistakes in the way they try to manage them.

There are two main ways you might deal with upsetting situations. I'll call them "helpful" and "hurtful." The helpful way means trying to do something about what is bothering you. It might take a few tries, but you keep at it. For example, suppose a fairly reasonable person annoys you. If he is blasting his radio and you can't study for a test, you might ask him to turn down the volume. However, if the person is someone you know who is mentally ill, you might remember from other occasions that this approach won't work. In that case another kind of action would be needed. You might read up on mental illness to see whether there are ways to get better cooperation from the person. You might also read about it just to find out why he is acting in this way and whether he can change his behavior.

You might discover that once you understand the reasons for the person's disturbing behavior, it is still just as annoying! You would then have to find ways of coping with it. Getting involved in after-school activities, in order to spend less time around the person, might be one way. Talking to a school counselor, just to get these heavy feelings off your chest rather than carry them around all the time, is another way. If you don't like how your parents are babying your mentally ill sister, or spending all their time taking care of Grandpa and ignoring you, you could talk to them about it and suggest how they

24

might act differently. In any case, you would admit your feelings to yourself and try to figure out if there is anything in your power that you can do about them. It takes a lot of guts to admit these feelings, and it often helps to have a psychologist or other trained person work with you.

As a psychologist, I've seen, too often, how young people use "hurtful" ways to avoid these negative feelings. The results can make things even worse. The following examples of what can happen if you avoid and hide from problems rather than work at solving them may remind you of yourself. If so, then it's not a minute too soon to look for some other ways of dealing with your emotions. Some kids try to put the feelings out of their minds by using drugs or alcohol. It seems easy, at first, just to drink or get high as a way of feeling better. The problem is that what's making you sad, angry, and so on doesn't go away. Then you have the original problem, plus all the problems that go along with using drugs or alcohol: your parents' anger, a drop in your grades, the risk of car accidents, and the danger of becoming addicted, to name a few.

Other kids, if they're feeling ignored, decide that they'll be able to get their parents' approval and attention by being perfect. They cook meals, clean the house, and work for all A's, hoping their parents will notice. If Mom and Dad don't notice, then they feel worse. Even if their parents do notice and approve, these efforts to be perfect can backfire. Kids can find that they're afraid to let up their hard work and relax for one minute. They can start to believe that unless they're perfect, no one will ever care about them.

Some kids show their feelings of anger or sadness in indirect, or hidden, ways. They might go from a B average in school to C's and D's or even F's. They might shoplift or cheat on tests, thinking, "That'll show them." Again, by not facing up to what is bothering them, they don't give the problem a chance to get solved. Some kids keep their feelings inside until they build to the level of an explosion. Then they scream and cry over what might be a small incident, such as their parent's forgetting to mail something for them. Or they might keep their feelings inside until they become depressed and feel hopeless that things can change for the better. Or they might act up in school, getting into fights and being rude to teachers, until their parents have to pay attention to them.

You can see why I said that how you deal with these feelings can affect your life in important ways.

In the next chapters I'll explain what the different types of mental illness are, what is known about their causes, and how they're treated. You may want to skip over these chapters for now if you've realized that your own ways of avoiding bad feelings are creating problems for you. You can go directly to chapters 10 and 11 instead and read about how you can help yourself and how you and other family members can help each other.

3

◆

Schizophrenia

Dear Lisa,

Sorry I haven't written to you in a while. Things have been totally weird! Remember my sister, Mary? She was only fourteen when you moved. She's seventeen now. Well, she's always been kind of quiet and private, but about a year ago she really started getting strange. She wouldn't talk to anyone at school, even the teachers—she just refused to answer in class! My mom had to talk to the principal about getting the teachers not to call on her, and about how she had gone to a psychologist but wouldn't cooperate. Anyway, Mary started staying in her room and eating meals there too. My dad gets so mad, he just blows his stack every once in a while, but it doesn't do any good. So then, a few weeks ago, Mary started talking to herself. Actually, she was talking to voices that no one else could hear. She almost set her room on fire, trying to hold a lit match, just because the voices told her to!

My parents didn't know what to do. My mom was crying every night. So finally, my mom and dad took her to this psychiatrist who said he'd have to evaluate her in the hospital, so she went there. We all went with her—that was the only way we could get her to go. I was so nervous. I had never seen a mental hospital before. Actually it was a psychiatric unit of a regular hospital, and it didn't look that bad, really. The patients didn't wear hospital gowns, just their regular clothes. Some of them didn't even look like there was anything wrong with them.

Mary was there for about two weeks. The doctor says she has schizophrenia—I couldn't believe it! It's not split personality like some people think. I feel so bad for her. We weren't that close, but she's helped me with chores and stuff and never even complained. I couldn't sleep the whole night after she went to the hospital, worrying about what will happen to her. I kept remembering how, when we were little, we'd play in the attic with old clothes and everything. Is she always going to be like this? Now she's taking medication, but she doesn't always want to take it, and I've seen Mom fight with her about it. I'm going to have to go to some family therapy meetings. In a way I don't want to go. Maybe they'll say it's something I did that made her turn out this way. But maybe I can find out why she acts the way she does.

It's really terrible. My grades are down in all my classes, and I can't concentrate. Before she went to the hospital, every time I came home I was afraid of what I would find. I can't even tell my friends at school about it. You're the only one outside my family I can tell. When my friends are over, they always look at her like she's weird. I just try to talk about something to get them not to notice her, but they do anyway. What if they think I'll catch it?

I don't believe this is happening. At least since the hospital she hasn't had any screaming matches with Mom or Dad about staying in her room all the time, so that's a relief. Mom was talking about getting a job to pay some of the doctor bills, which means I'll have more stuff to do around here. I keep thinking, maybe I'll wake up and it will all be just a bad dream. Anyway, I'd better go. I have tons of work for school. Write soon! Maybe I can come live with you!

Love,
Carla

30

What Is Schizophrenia?

If someone in your family has schizophrenia, certain symptoms led to that diagnosis. These are probably quite familiar to you, even if the doctor's words for them sound complicated. "Deterioration in functioning," "delusions," "hallucinations," "inappropriate emotions"—it's hard to connect these words with the disturbing behavior you've been observing. Perhaps you've seen someone you care about just stop studying or going to work and instead start hiding out in a bedroom or finished basement. Maybe you've tried to convince someone that the words coming out of the radio aren't a personal message from God. You may have watched the person cry for no reason or laugh at sad parts of a TV movie. Or you've listened to someone talk out loud to voices that no one else hears. All of these are the kinds of behaviors that doctors look for in deciding if someone has schizophrenia. Since symptoms such as these must be present for at least six months before a diagnosis of schizophrenia is made, you've no doubt been trying to cope with these upsetting and unpredictable kinds of behavior for some time now.

In order to understand schizophrenia, it's helpful

to look beyond the obvious symptoms. If you could peek inside the person's head, the odd and frightening behavior you've been witnessing wouldn't be quite as confusing. As surprising as it seems, this behavior makes a kind of sense from the viewpoint of the person with schizophrenia. People who have this illness have said that in the early stages of a schizophrenic breakdown, colors seem brighter and sounds seem sharper. Most of us can automatically ignore wallpaper designs, traffic noises outside the window, and other unimportant parts of our surroundings. The person with schizophrenia can't do this, because every object grabs her attention equally.

In a world where familiar or important people and things no longer stand out against a background, the person tries to give meaning to these experiences. No wonder she comes up with some pretty strange—to others—ideas to explain what's happening. Considering that the usual rules of everyday life have been turned inside out, perhaps it's reasonable for her to believe that the FBI is following her! The strange and unexpected bombardment of sights and sounds brings on a variety of emotions. Naturally, these emotional reactions look unpredictable and bizarre to other people, based, as

32

they are, on unusual experiences inside the person's head. In this situation, doesn't it make sense, in a way, that this person is acting strangely? Her brain is playing tricks on her that she couldn't stop, even if she tried.

In Mary's case, the symptoms didn't suddenly appear one day. As with most people who are eventually diagnosed as schizophrenic, a much more gradual process took place. Mary's parents and sister considered her shyness and lack of confidence during grade school to be "just her nature." They would have liked Mary to be more outgoing, as her sister Carla was, but nothing they did to encourage her in social activities worked. Efforts to have her invite other girls over to play usually ended up with Mary and her playmate fighting and Mary going off to her room. By junior high, Mary was pulling back more and more from the social whirl of "best friends" and "who likes who." Spending most of her time alone with her thoughts and away from classmates, she missed out on chances to learn the "in" words or how to tell the difference between mean and friendly teasing. No wonder the cycle continued downward: distrust of other kids, keeping to herself, teasing by the kids, more distrust, and so on. When Mary refused to go to the dances after school, her parents tried to reassure each other that she was just a "late bloomer."

Mary also kept to herself at home, reading about pollution and drawing pictures of inventions to make the world clean. At school she dared not say a word to the girls who called her names, but at home, when her parents or sister raised doubts or questions about her actions, she would run, screaming, to her room. After these incidents she became more and more secretive at home. As the outbursts came more often, her parents took her to a psychologist, but Mary wouldn't share her secret thoughts and fantasies, so the attempt at counseling lasted only three weeks. It was not until her senior year of high school, after years of growing suspiciousness and isolation, that the full symptoms of schizophrenia appeared. By the time she started hearing voices and answering them, the earlier oddness could be put into perspective as the beginning of schizophrenia.

Some people's symptoms appear to develop more suddenly. In his book *The Eden Express,* about his experience with schizophrenia, Mark Vonnegut described the frightening sensations he had shortly before his illness was diagnosed. He was part of the sixties' "hippie generation," and drug experimentation apparently played a part in bringing on his symptoms.

> And from out of nowhere came an incredibly wrinkled, iridescent face. Starting as a small point infinitely distant, it rushed forward, becoming infinitely huge. I could see nothing else. . . . I lay rigid all night listening to the sounds of the stream, figuring that somehow by being aware of sounds and rhythms out-side myself I could keep my own bodily rhythms going. Losing consciousness of something outside myself meant that I would die.

Mark Vonnegut's thoughts, feelings, and behav-ior were outside the limits of reality. The strange face he saw, and his fears of his body shutting down, naturally led to behavior that looked strange to oth-ers. These symptoms are typical of schizophrenia. Interestingly, he realized at times that perhaps he was going "insane," but he was unable to stop the process.

If you're living with someone who has schizophre-nia, you may well wonder what is likely to happen to the person in the years ahead. According to E. F.

Torrey, a psychiatrist who has studied this disease, a "rule of thirds" says that about one-third of schizophrenics will get completely well, one-third will improve to some degree, and one-third will not improve. Since this "rule" is based on studies of what happens to groups of patients, it's impossible to know exactly how a particular person's illness will turn out. The future outcome does seem to be related to the person's past history. That is, the younger and less well adjusted a person was before the initial breakdown, and the more relapses a person has had, the less likely that person is to recover.

What this means for you is that if your brother began showing clear signs of schizophrenia at age sixteen, with a past history of odd behavior and no friendships, plus several hospitalizations by the time he was twenty, his chances of recovering fully are small. If this is the case, you and your family will have many adjustments to make, as well as plans for his future care and treatment. On the other hand, if your thirty-eight-year-old mother has had one or two episodes of schizophrenia, each lasting less than a year, since she was thirty years old, she has an excellent chance of making a complete recovery. Of course, no matter what your relative's history has been, your family will want to make sure to provide the best possible care.

36

Suspected Causes of Schizophrenia

You have probably wondered what can cause these strange and upsetting symptoms. If it's a sister or brother who has schizophrenia, does that mean you'll be the next to get it? Did the disease come from something your parents did in trying to raise him or her? Since the early 1900s people in the mental health field have tried to explain schizophrenia in terms of disturbed family relationships. Yet studies of parents whose children developed schizophrenia haven't been very useful in discovering its causes. Although we don't know for sure what causes this disease, some research findings appear to be pointed in the right direction. What does seem clear now is that there are differences between the brains of people with schizophrenia and those without it. One of the theories about what causes these differences has to do with genes handed down from earlier generations; another suggests slow-acting viruses that may have infected the person early in childhood or even in the womb. These theories are still being tested. Perhaps a lack of certain vitamins or other nutrients could be involved, although this theory is probably the most controversial. In some cases severe and prolonged stress could be the cause. There are even some people who believe that schizophrenia is really several different diseases with similar symptoms, each with its own separate cause.

Someday in the future, perhaps the cause or causes will be definitively known. Meanwhile, much is still to be learned about the exact way in which schizophrenia develops. Fortunately, there has been progress in the treatment of the disease even without a perfect understanding of its causes.

Hospitals and Schizophrenia

Schizophrenia can be treated either in a hospital or on an outpatient basis, with visits to a mental health professional one or two times a week, perhaps less often in later stages. Chances are, your family member with schizophrenia has been in a hospital at least once because of the illness. There are several reasons for this.

If you can recall the beginnings of your relative's schizophrenia, the strange symptoms probably reached a point where immediate attention and thorough evaluation were needed. Usually the family gets frightened by the serious errors of reality that the person is making, or they feel they or the person are in danger of being injured. Mary had hallucinations (voices that weren't there) and delusions (strange ideas), and the unusual behavior that followed from these almost resulted in a fire. Although her symptoms were typical of schizophrenia, the doctor may have felt that possibly some other type of illness was responsible. Sometimes drugs or other abnormal conditions affecting the brain can cause symptoms that are confusingly similar to those of schizophrenia. In order to make sure of a correct diagnosis, then, Mary was brought to a hospital, where she could be observed and laboratory tests could rule out other problems. Perhaps a similar set of events occurred in your family.

Taking Mary to the hospital was frightening for her family. On the way Mary's mother remembered stories she used to hear about an aunt who was in a mental hospital. People in the family would send Christmas and birthday cards, but they avoided visiting the aunt because her odd behavior made them uncomfortable. All Mary's parents knew about mental hospitals was what they had seen in old movies, TV shows, and magazines. They recalled images of patients in padded cells (small rooms with walls of thick padding) and straitjackets (white garments with long sleeves that wrapped around to the person's back, preventing use of the arms), devices for controlling their sometimes dangerous behavior.

Memories of these scenes made Mary's parents feel guilty about taking their daughter to the hospital. Carla knew even less than her parents did about mental hospitals, but her imagination created equally scary pictures in her mind. The drastic step of hospitalizing Mary meant that Mary's parents and sister had to face the possibility that she had a serious mental illness. Would Mary spend years in the hospital, as her mother's aunt had?

Chances are, in your own family, each person has had different feelings about when and whether to take the ill person to the hospital. Guilt about "dumping" the person in the hospital, worry about what might happen if the person stayed home, and relief once the person was in someone else's care are all common emotions that you and your family have probably experienced.

Hospitals can help by protecting both the family and the person with schizophrenia. Sometimes the ill person's disturbed thinking has made him want to kill himself or hurt other people. Perhaps you have seen how your relative's schizophrenia has kept him from being safe, even if actual violence hasn't been a concern. He may try to drive a car while distracted by voices or refuse to eat because he fears that all food is poisoned. Mark Vonnegut wasn't threatening or dangerous to himself or others at the time of

40

his first hospitalization. Yet his ability to take care of his most basic needs for food, shelter, and clothing had decreased to the point where hospitalization was necessary for his survival. The feeling of relief to the rest of the family when their ill relative is in the safety of a hospital can, at least in part, make up for the feelings of guilt and sadness that went along with the hospitalization.

Drugs and Their Limitations

After talking to the doctor who would be caring for Mary, her parents and sister were relieved to know that medications, called neuroleptics or antipsychotics, could calm Mary and even stop the hallucinations and delusions. Because antipsychotic medications don't affect all patients in exactly the same way, finding the right medication and dose takes time. Treating Mary in the hospital gave her doctor the chance to observe her reactions and make sure that the medication was helping.

It is likely that antipsychotic medications are an important part of your relative's treatment. They help the person re-enter the real world and allow brief hospitalizations rather than years of confinement. These drugs have also made the old methods of controlling dangerous behavior unnecessary for

41

most people. In spite of these definite benefits, you may already be aware of some of the drawbacks. Some side effects, such as dry mouth, are minor and go away in a few weeks. Others, such as restlessness and stiffness, may be more disturbing to the patient. Even if they aren't serious, the patient may be troubled enough by them to choose to stop taking the medication. Or your family may be frightened by the stories about the most serious side effect, tardive dyskinesia, which consists of involuntary sucking, chewing, and smacking movements of the mouth. If the doctor who is treating your relative watches for signs of this disorder, the medication can be stopped or the dosage can be lowered before the problem becomes severe or permanent. Yet some families are so worried about this possible side effect that they may refuse treatment with these drugs, resulting in a return of the symptoms. Other families believe, correctly, that a lower dose of medication could be equally effective and have fewer side effects than the dose their family member is taking.

A major limitation of the drugs is that they do not cure the disease. As a result, relapses in schizophrenia are not unusual after the first diagnosis. This fact of life is one of the most difficult parts of having someone with schizophrenia in your family. If your relative had diabetes, for example, and wasn't careful about taking insulin, the bad effects would hurt mainly himself. If your relative with schizophrenia stops taking the medication, however, the effects are serious for everyone in the family. The strange and frightening behavior and the unpredictable disruptions of your life will gradually return, until perhaps only another hospitalization convinces the patient that the medication is necessary. Even with medication, relapses can occur.

When Mark Vonnegut was first hospitalized, his symptoms responded fairly quickly to antipsychotic medication. However, it was hard for him, as it is for many people with schizophrenia, to believe that he was truly ill. Eager to leave the hospital, Vonnegut convinced a doctor to discharge him. Released without any plans for follow-up treatment, it was just a matter of weeks before he experienced a return of the symptoms, and another trip to the hospital became necessary.

Other Treatments

If your relative has been in the hospital, then in addition to starting on medication, she has probably been involved in other kinds of treatment with hospital staff. The nurses on a psychiatric unit play an important role in allowing your family member the chance to talk about what has happened to her and in making sure that she keeps to a routine of activities. Therapy groups for recognizing and expressing feelings through music or art may be available and helpful.

Another part of the treatment for schizophrenia is psychotherapy, the talking and problem solving that take place during visits to a psychologist or other mental health professional. After Mary's first schizophrenic breakdown, she continued to go back to the hospital every week to talk with her psychiatrist about her feelings concerning her illness and other problems she was having. Learning ways to handle stress, and developing a trusting relationship with her doctor, helped Mary. She began to realize that it was possible to cope with what she felt was a lack of understanding by other people in her life. Over many months, not just weeks, she was able to accept that she had schizophrenia and find ways to live with it. She also started gradually to become independent of her parents and eventually was able to start attending a community college part time.

Family therapy is often used in addition to individual psychotherapy in treating people with schizophrenia. This therapy can take place during hospitalization and later on an outpatient basis. If

you are involved in family therapy with your relative, you've seen that it gives you and other family
members a chance to learn and talk about how you
can help one another and the ill person in your
family. It's another important part of your whole
family's adjustment to the stress of mental illness.
Perhaps your ill family member finds these family
sessions too upsetting and does not attend, or at-
tends only some. Even so, attending the sessions
can give you, your parents, and other close family
members the help you need in learning how to live
with someone who has schizophrenia.

In family therapy you can talk about what it was
like before your family member was diagnosed and
how things are now. Your anger and frustration with
someone who seemed disagreeable or even purposely annoying may have made you say some
things that you now remember with a lot of guilt.
You may have argued with your parents about how
much time they were spending trying to help the
sick person while you struggled with your own problems. These arguments may still be happening, or
they may be an unpleasant memory that keeps you
and your parents from getting along as well as you'd
like. The therapist can help you all find better ways
of dealing with your disagreements. Since your relative may at times refuse to take medication or to

attend therapy sessions of her own, your fears and worries about what will happen when the symptoms return can also be discussed in family therapy. Finding ways to relax during calm periods while still being aware that the peace may be shattered at any time can be helpful to you in getting on with your own life.

It's important to remember that someone with schizophrenia doesn't always have the delusions and hallucinations that may have first brought her to treatment. Between those episodes of obviously psychotic behavior are times of relative calm, referred to as residual schizophrenia. The person may still have trouble thinking logically, relating well to others, and having the normal range of emotions. In addition to the family and individual psychotherapy that may be needed, during these periods patients often benefit from programs that concentrate on social and vocational rehabilitation. Getting along with people and handling job demands are important skills that can increase self-esteem and help the person stay out of the hospital. This type of progress can relieve some of the stress on family members, who find it hard to see a person of average or above average intelligence that they care about just sitting in her room all day, doing nothing.

46

Commitment

One of the most difficult situations your family may face could come if your relative's behavior became a danger to himself or other people. If he refused to go into a hospital for treatment, the family might need to have him hospitalized against his will. This procedure is called commitment. The laws that tell how a person can be committed and under what circumstances are different from state to state. In general, though, a doctor can usually sign a paper that allows the person to be placed in the hospital for about three days. In order to keep him there for a longer period, a legal procedure in front of a judge or other official is generally necessary. An attorney will be appointed for the schizophrenic person to make sure that his legal rights are not overlooked.

If your family member has needed hospitalization but refused to go, you may remember very clearly how frustrating it is to go through the legal steps that are required. After all, what could be wrong with putting someone in the hospital as a precaution against his hurting himself or someone else? You may be surprised to know that for many years the legal rights of patients were given no attention at all. As a result of lawsuits by concerned citizens and others, it was learned that some people were kept in mental institutions for many years longer than necessary, often without treatment. The recent concern for patients' rights has changed things to the point that in many situations patients can have the right to refuse treatment. The new approach has helped people who may have had their rights ignored in the past to get the treatment they need and to be released when they are ready. On the other hand, families who have not been able to get their ill relative committed when they believed it was necessary have felt frustrated and worried as a result.

Even if your family has been able to have a member committed to a hospital in an emergency, the result has probably not been completely happy. You and your parents may have felt relief at not being around the disturbed and disturbing behavior and at knowing that your family member was in safe surroundings. You probably had other feelings as well. In particular, guilt over having to put a family member in the hospital without his consent may have made you and the rest of your family wonder if you have done the right thing. You and your parents may have argued, if you felt they were wrong to go through with a commitment proceeding. This may have left you feeling frustrated and helpless. Your ill relative may have been angry about the commitment, resulting in awkward and tense moments during visits or after his release. Making decisions about treatment and having to live with them can be one of the hardest parts of having a family member with schizophrenia.

Deinstitutionalization

Because of greater awareness of patients' rights and because of the effectiveness of antipsychotic medications, a treatment practice called deinstitutionalization has come about, with both good and bad results. This has affected many people with schizophrenia, including, most likely, your ill family member. This approach means that more and more patients are being treated in the community rather than spending long periods of time in mental hospitals. Unlike the mentally ill aunt in Mary's family, who was sometimes whispered about and was remembered only at holiday time, Mary will probably be familiar to all of her relatives. They might know her as someone who is a little different or who gets ill from time to time, but perhaps they won't have the fear that Mary's mother had about what it is to be mentally ill.

Deinstitutionalization has created its own problems, however. Laws passed by Congress in the

1960s required that clinics called Community Mental Health Centers were to be set up all over the country. These CMHC's (for short) are supposed to provide mental health services to people who need them, with the cost of treatment adjusted according to the person's or family's income. As a result of the newer focus on outpatient treatment, many mental hospitals have closed. Yet many families of the mentally ill have felt that seriously ill people, such as those with schizophrenia, have not been given the opportunity to make use of these CMHC's. For example, suppose your family member's doctor has made arrangements for him to continue treatment at a CMHC after leaving the hospital, and your family finds that the CMHC has a long waiting list? Many mentally ill people, especially those who may have moved away from their families and have no one helping them, can get lost in the system. As a result, patients and their families have felt angry and frustrated that no one is looking out for their needs.

Among the disadvantages of inpatient treatment are the high costs and the difficulty, for patients, of the transition from a hospital to outpatient treatment. New treatment alternatives have been developed to deal with these concerns. You and your family may have worried about how your relative would cope with leaving the around-the-clock care of a hospital and going home. Questions of who is responsible for making sure medication is taken and therapy appointments are kept have probably come up. Day treatment is a type of program designed to ease the transition. Some hospitals have set aside areas where former inpatients can come during the day and participate in therapy groups and other helpful activities. In the evening they return home. In this way, the support and protective surroundings of the hospital are not suddenly exchanged for complete independence, which can be too much for the person to handle. Another type of program is a halfway house. The person with schizophrenia lives in a homelike building with other former hospital patients who are mentally ill. Counselors are on hand to give help in polishing job application skills and learning other requirements of independent living. If your family has tried to get your relative into day treatment or a halfway house, you may have found that the big problem with both of these types of programs is that there aren't enough of them.

If your mentally ill relative has been discharged from a hospital but has been unable to participate in a program such as day treatment or a halfway house, then you know the troubles that often follow. He may move back home, leaving you and other family members to deal with odd or disturbing behavior. He may start out well, but then slack off in taking medication or following through with psychotherapy sessions. He may find family members' interest in him and their efforts to help too much to deal with. He may just take off suddenly, leaving you and your family worried about where and how he is.

Probably the most important thing you can do if someone in your family has schizophrenia is to become involved in a support group for families of the mentally ill. By joining this type of group, you can meet other people who are struggling with the same sorts of problems you have as a result of having a mentally ill person in your family. You can ask your parents or the mental health professional who is helping your relative to tell you how to join. If they are not able to put you in touch with an organization, there are addresses in the back of this book. You can contact them on your own if necessary.

It can be said that schizophrenia is the most serious mental illness. Living with a person who has it can at times make you feel as if you are on an emotional roller coaster. Learning all you can about the disease and how to cope with it is not just a choice but a necessity.

4

◆

Mood Disorders

MY FAMILY, BY JESSICA H.

In my family, there's me, my brother Todd, my mom, and my dad. My brother is cool. He plays football at the high school. I like to watch him play. He calls girls on the phone a lot, and they call him, too. I get mad when I can't use the phone.

My dad is very nice. He lives two miles from us. He works for the phone company. He likes to fix things. He made me a bookcase for my room. He tries to do fun things with me and Todd on weekends. He wishes Todd and me could come and live with him.

My mom is nice. In the morning she hates to get up. Todd gives me breakfast. Sometimes we ask her to take us to the roller rink, but she doesn't feel like it. Todd gets mad when she won't go. I feel sad.

NOTHING TO BE ASHAMED OF

Mom says she might go to our third grade concert.
I hope so.

Todd blinked back tears as he read Jessica's school paper. So much that she could have said was left out. Like the way she prayed every night before bedtime that Mom would get better. Or the way she turned down a birthday party for herself this year, because it wouldn't be fun with Mom depressed the way she was. She wouldn't even celebrate her birthday at Dad's house because Mom wasn't happy. Todd had tried to explain to Jessica that she was allowed to be happy even if Mom wasn't, but it didn't help.

Todd's feelings shifted from anger to despair to what's-the-use. He knew from the other times that Mom would get back to her old self after a while. But when she did, there was always the worry that she'd get depressed again.

Even though Dad had moved out three years ago, Dad and Mom still weren't divorced, and Dad tried to help out in a crisis. Money would be tight for a while. Todd hoped he could get his driver's license soon, so he could take Mom to her doctor's appointments until she was able to drive herself. That way Dad wouldn't have to miss work.

What Is Depression?

Depression is one of a group of mental illnesses called mood disorders. People with these disorders have disturbances in their mood that are serious enough to interrupt their everyday lives.

Like everyone else, you've probably had times when you've felt very sad or "down." Perhaps someone you loved was sick, or even died. Or a best friend stopped being nice to you. It may have taken days or weeks, but sooner or later you got back to your old routine, even if at times the sadness came back briefly. You may also have had the experience of being on a "high" for a few days after something really exciting happened. Suppose your football team won the league or state championship, or you won an important prize. You probably stayed up late, too excited to sleep, and you talked about the good news over and over. These ups and downs are normal reactions to events in your life. They go away on their own after a while, unlike the problems called mood disorders.

Some people, like Todd's mother, go through one or more periods of serious depression. Todd was ten when his mother first became depressed. It seemed to him then that his mother had pulled away from the family. She would lie in bed late into the morning. She hardly touched her food, and she had lost interest in shopping or cooking for Todd, two-year-old Jessica, and their dad. She seemed to go through the motions of caring for Jessica, without the playfulness or fun that Jessica was used to. Their dad had to go in late to work so he could give Jessica her breakfast. Then he'd call home a few times a day to make sure Jessica was being fed and taken care of.

It was hard for Todd, Jessica, and their dad to understand what was happening to this seeming stranger in their family. They couldn't see that the former PTA president and Cub Scout den mother could only think of herself as a horrible failure. They didn't understand that the small amount of energy it took them to get dressed or comb their hair seemed impossibly out of reach to her. They couldn't imagine that the obvious step of going to a doctor to find out what was wrong seemed more challenging than climbing Mt. Everest. Instead Todd and his dad tried to fight their feelings of anger, hurt, and sorrow. They knew there had to be something wrong with Mom, but without the specific complaints or clear signs of a physical illness, they found it hard to be sympathetic.

When Todd was in junior high, arguments between his parents finally led to his father's moving out. Even now, Todd couldn't help wondering if his mother's depressions had caused the separation. If she hadn't been depressed, would his parents have gotten along better? On the other hand, if they had argued less, would his mother not have become depressed? It was all so confusing. Unfortunately there was no way to answer those questions.

Although Todd would have liked to live with his dad, he felt he couldn't desert his mother. At the same time, he resented feeling responsible for her. His grades started to slip and his teachers noticed that his attitude toward school had changed for the worse. Fortunately his school psychologist was able to help him find better ways of coping with his upset feelings before he got too far behind in his schoolwork.

Not all people with depression are like Todd's mother. Instead of feeling drained of all their energy, some people become agitated or restless and pace back and forth, wringing their hands. There are also people who sleep and eat much more than usual, rather than less. In extreme cases a depressed person may become psychotic, with delusions that she has killed or poisoned someone, for example.

Bipolar Disorder

A smaller group of people with mood disorders have more to deal with than depression. They must also contend with its opposite. They become excited and energetic and are bursting with ideas of grand projects to tackle. At first their high spirits and enthusiasm may impress the people around them, making them almost envious. Before long, though, people realize that the person's thinking has crossed the line between what's realistic and what is not, and his goals have passed the boundary between ambitious and dangerous. One challenge for family members is to control the damage that can occur if the person goes forward with his plans. Someone with big decorating ideas might take a sledgehammer and start knocking down the walls of his living room!

Jennifer's parents sometimes needed to keep an eye on her grandmother, to make sure she didn't spend herself into debt. Jennifer's grandmother usually was able to live and work without problems, while taking medication for her disorder. Occasionally she stopped the medication, against the advice of her doctor. Within weeks she would become talkative and excited. She'd come home to her apartment with huge packages from the department store, having charged jewelry, furs, and other luxuries on her credit card. If her daughter, Jennifer's mother, tried to suggest that she was spending too much, she'd become angry. She would call her daughter insulting names and hang up the phone. Even more upsetting than the purchases, Grandma would behave in a way she'd ordinarily consider immoral. She flirted with men she didn't know, in stores and restaurants and on the street, and invited them to her apartment. Jennifer's mother worried about what might happen if Grandma got involved with someone who could be dangerous or take advantage of her.

The name *bipolar* for this disorder refers to the fact that the person's mood shifts between two "poles" or extremes, from manic to depressed. For most people who have this illness, months or years can go by between disturbed periods. In rare cases manic and depressive episodes alternate as often as several times a year. Depending on the degree of excitement, a person can be diagnosed as hypomanic (mildly manic) or manic. In extreme cases the person becomes psychotic, with false ideas and hallucinations similar to the schizophrenic's. In fact, it can be difficult for a doctor to be sure, at first, whether someone is manic or schizophrenic when this occurs.

Causes of Mood Disorders

Scientists are looking into family illness patterns and brain chemistry to understand the causes of mood disorders, just as they are for schizophrenia. Many studies have been done on families of people with mood disorders. Although the family studies don't prove the cause of a disorder, they do give researchers clues to follow in deciding where to look further. As is true of schizophrenia, someone with a mood disorder will usually have relatives who also have or had it. It's important to remind yourself that having a relative who is depressed or manic-depressive doesn't guarantee you will develop the disorder.

While Todd's mother was being diagnosed as having a major depression, the family learned that Todd's great-grandfather and a great-aunt had also suffered from depression. Todd and his father had never heard about either of these people until they asked Todd's grandmother about the family health history. She recalled that her father had gone through several depressions. Over the years she had pushed aside this memory and the shame she had felt as a teenager. Her father's tearful mood during those times had always embarrassed her. Even worse, the fact that he had taken "shock treatments" was something her whole family had tried to forget.

Family history, important as it is, doesn't really explain what happens when mood disorders occur. Research on the exact causes has focused on certain parts of the brain and the chemicals that allow these parts to send messages to one another. We know that normal mood changes, from happiness to sorrow, are controlled by these chemicals. Experiments are indicating that too much or too little of these chemicals plays a part in bringing on depression or mania. Research has also revealed that stresses can actually cause changes in the body that throw these chemicals out of balance. Losing a loved one is among the many types of stress that can have this effect.

Knowing what stress does can be helpful to you if you have a depressed person in your family. If you know that your father's side of the family has a history of heart disease, you can try to eat healthy foods, exercise, and not smoke, to avoid or lessen your own risk of heart disease. In much the same way, you can improve your resistance to depression or mania by learning to recognize and cope with stresses in your life. Although there are some cases of mood disorders that come on without any clear-cut stresses, stress can bring on depression in someone who's at risk because of family history.

Other studies show that the "internal clocks" that control everyone's sleeping and waking periods may be disturbed in people with depression. People's biological reactions to changes in the seasons may also be important, since depression is most common in spring and fall. Because so many people are affected by depression, research is sure to continue in order to help us understand this disorder better.

Medications for Depression

During Todd's mother's first depression Todd and his dad spent three weeks urging, pleading, and begging before they convinced her to go to her doctor for a checkup. Since many physical illnesses and some medications can make a person seem depressed, the doctor ordered tests to make sure that some hidden condition wasn't responsible for her symptoms. When the results were negative, the doctor recommended that she see a psychiatrist.

Dr. Mendez was able to see Todd's mother the next day. She asked Todd's mother about her childhood and her family, her present situation, and how she had been feeling. Based on the answers, Dr. Mendez told Todd's mother that she was experienc-

62

ing a major (that is, serious) depression. The doctor then asked whether she had been thinking that her life wasn't worth living. After satisfying herself that her new patient wasn't about to commit suicide, Dr. Mendez said that she would prescribe an antidepressant medication. Unfortunately, it would take at least three to four weeks before the medication would start to lift the depression. During that time she would see Todd's mother twice each week.

Like schizophrenia, depression is often treated with medications. Depending on the specific medication, side effects can include dry mouth, blurred vision, and drowsiness. Other types of antidepressants cause serious side effects if certain foods are eaten, requiring strict limits on these foods. For reasons that aren't clear, each type of antidepressant doesn't work equally well for everyone. Although the doctor will first prescribe a medication with the least bothersome side effects and limitations, the main goal is to find one that works for each person.

The antidepressant medication Todd's mother took began to bring improvement in her sleeping, her energy level, and finally her mood. About four weeks after she first saw Dr. Mendez, she felt much better. After two more months she was able to taper off and then stop the medication. Yet the experience of seeing her so depressed made her family continue to worry that she might get depressed again.

By the time Todd was in high school, his mother was in her third major depression. Each time it took a while before she would go back for treatment. In the meantime Todd, Jessica, and their father became frustrated with Mom's lack of energy and hopeless appearance. They hated seeing her pull back from the family and feel that she was no good. Even though getting her to the doctor and paying for treatment was difficult, it was still better than seeing her refuse help.

To the family's surprise, a more effective use of antidepressant medication emerged during the latest episode of depression. Rather than relying on how well Todd's mother felt and looked, or on the recommended dosage, the doctor had her take blood tests several times to make sure that she was getting a high enough dose to make a real difference. Each person's body uses medication a little differently, so a blood test is the most accurate way to know if the person is getting enough. Once Todd's mom was feeling a lot better, the doctor had her continue taking the medication until additional tests showed that the depression was really gone. It was only after going through two earlier depressions that Todd's mother was able to get the treatment she needed to prevent future relapses.

Although it may seem simple to take some pills and get over being depressed, it's important to remember that there are many complicating factors. Some people don't respond to antidepressant medications. Others have trouble accepting the side effects and stop taking the medication before it has a chance to help lift the depression, or they simply stop the medication before the needed chemical changes in the brain take place. After all, haven't most of us forgotten or not bothered to take a pill or follow instructions that will help us? Someone who is depressed has an especially hard time believing that the prescribed treatment will do any good. Many depressed people avoid going to a mental health professional. Others who do go aren't helped by antidepressants because they are actually on too low a dose to show improvement.

Psychotherapies for Depression

Medication isn't the only treatment for depression. Psychotherapy is equally necessary. Perhaps you've been involved in your family member's individual psychotherapy, or in family therapy. Not only

65

can it be helpful to the depressed person, it can also give you a chance to express your needs and have them satisfied.

An important type of psychotherapy for depression is called cognitive therapy. Studies of this treatment have found it to be as effective as medication. It is based on the idea that depressed people have thoughts about themselves and the world that make them depressed. They may think "I'm no good," or "Nobody likes me." They accept these thoughts as fact, without question. The cognitive therapist works with depressed people on attacking and disproving these thoughts and on finding more useful ways to look at their lives. Usually a specific number of sessions is planned for going through the steps of the treatment.

Another psychotherapy used for treating depressed people is called interpersonal therapy. In this approach the person works on improving relationships with different people in her life. The focus is on the person's current situation, not on things that happened long ago.

A combination of antidepressant medication and psychotherapy is often used to treat depression. The medication can quickly help the person get to the point where she has the energy and hopefulness needed for trying to solve problems in her life. The psychotherapist can help the person change the thought patterns that could bring on future depressions and learn to deal with stresses in more useful ways.

Electroconvulsive Therapy

Another treatment for depression is electroconvulsive therapy (ECT), which used to be called shock treatment. Since the development of antidepressants, ECT isn't used as much as it was in the past. This treatment involves giving the person a mild electric shock, which triggers a seizure. Unlike the seizure of someone with epilepsy, which happens unexpectedly, the shock is given under careful medical supervision, so that the person is not in any danger of being injured. For reasons that aren't clear, ECT does seem effective in lifting depression. Yet because it seems so drastic and frightening, many people are opposed to its use. ECT can be particularly valuable for people who haven't had success with other treatments or who can't take medications for some reason. It also gets results more quickly than antidepressant medication, which makes it helpful for suicidal patients.

The main side effects of ECT are confusion and headache immediately after the treatment, and memory loss that may last a month. Because specially trained people are needed to make sure the ECT is done safely, the treatment is given in the hospital.

Treatment of Bipolar Disorder

Since the 1970s a type of mineral salt called lithium has been used both to treat manic patients and to prevent relapses. For Jennifer's grandmother, the discovery of lithium treatment made a huge difference. She was able to work at her job as manager of a clothing store without being disrupted by periods of overexcitement or depression. Yet, at times, Grandma missed the highs of her manic phases and stopped taking the lithium. She also grew tired of the occasional blood tests she needed to make sure that she wasn't getting too much lithium, which can be harmful.

As with other medications, side effects can occur with lithium. Thirst, fatigue, and stomach upset may last only a few days, but hand tremors, weight gain, and other symptoms may last longer. The doctor can lessen these side effects by changing the dosage or prescribing other medications. Once again, the usefulness of the medication in helping the person lead a normal life must be weighed against the discomfort of the side effects.

Risk of Suicide

The most serious outcome of a depression is suicide. Depression keeps a person from seeing that a better, happier life is possible. The person focuses on the terrible things in his life and is unable to look at the "bright side." It's as if the person were wearing blinders, seeing only part of the picture. For these reasons a depressed person may decide that the only way to stop feeling bad is to end his life. If a person has actually tried to kill himself, hospitalization is clearly needed. If he is talking about it or showing other signs of wanting to die, family members need to be sure the person is evaluated by a mental health professional. He may need to go to the hospital until medication or psychotherapy helps him see that his life is worth living.

The topic of suicide is scary for family members. You may wonder, "When should I be concerned about it?" The answer is: any time a person is seriously depressed. You or other family members may feel helpless about discussing it with the person. You may be afraid that asking if he has thoughts of

69

suicide will give him the idea. People in the mental health field have found that this is not what happens. Someone who's very depressed actually may be relieved to have a chance to talk about these feelings. Usually the person doesn't have a clear, one-sided wish to die. Instead, he has some feelings that are keeping him from trying it. If he is a parent, he may want to live to see his children grow up. He may be hoping that someone will see how truly unhappy he is and do something to help. By asking about those thoughts and showing that you are concerned, you can tip the balance toward the "living" side of the scale. When Todd's mother was asked if she had thoughts of suicide, she was relieved that the doctor could understand how deep her feeling of hopelessness was. If you feel you should bring up this subject with your family member but you're not sure how to do it, it's important to get help. Asking your doctor, a school counselor, or another adult is the best place to start.

Suppose you do get up the courage to ask the person if he has thought about suicide, and the person admits that he can't see any other way out? In that case you need help right away, from a parent or other adult family member, in getting the person into a hospital. The problem is bigger than you or anyone can handle alone. Committing a person to a hospital against his will is upsetting to family members, but sometimes it's the only way to prevent a person from killing himself. Remember that the person may be unable to see his situation clearly. If depression is keeping him from seeing other alternatives to dying, getting him to treatment is the most important step you and your family can take.

It's hard for family members not to worry about suicide. In a sense, worrying that someone who is depressed will commit suicide is like worrying that a family member who has had a heart attack or stroke will have another one. You wouldn't expect that you could prevent a heart attack or stroke. One of the most difficult things about dealing with a mentally ill person is that the person has thoughts and feelings that stem from the illness. It may not be easy for you and other family members to realize that persuading, nagging, or reasoning are about as useful in stopping the depressed thoughts and feelings as they would be in preventing a heart attack. Just as in cases where a relative has a serious physical illness, there are several things you can do to help, other than worrying. Encouraging the person to follow the treatment program, making it easier in whatever way you can for the person to continue treatment, and showing that you care and will listen are the most valuable things you can do. Anything else is beyond your control.

Sadly, there are people who do manage to kill themselves. Losing a relative to suicide leaves family members hurt, angry, and confused. "How could he do this to me?" "I should have prevented it." "There's nothing I can do to help now." These are all typical thoughts after a suicide. If this has happened in your family, it's important to talk about it with other family members. There are also support groups for people in your situation. Although the hurt is often too strong to put into words right after the suicide, months later you may be more able to face it and talk about it. Many of your friends and classmates may have trouble talking to you about your mentally ill family member; they may have even more difficulty knowing what to say in the case of suicide. A support group is sometimes the only place where you can let out these feelings with people who understand.

The most important thing to remember is that neither you nor anyone else can follow someone around all the time to prevent him from killing himself. No one can be responsible for keeping another person alive in that way. Although you may carry a lump of sadness in your heart for the person who died, you don't have to add to it the guilt of feeling that you should have prevented the death.

Living with someone who has a mood disorder can make you upset or perhaps actually depressed. Even when you can understand what is happening and why your family member is feeling this way, the disruptions to your life may continue. For that reason, getting help for yourself is important. Whether your goal is to talk about, or "unload," all the things that are bothering you, to find ways to cope with them, or to make sure that you're not slipping into a serious depression yourself, some visits with a mental health professional are definitely worth the time, effort, and even cost.

5

◆

Anxiety Disorders

Allison tossed the invitation into her special box. "Save the date! October 31 . . ." She didn't bother to read any more, other than to notice it was from Tom in her geometry class. "Probably a Halloween party," she thought. The special box held other invitations collected over several years: birthday parties, Bar Mitzvahs, confirmation parties. Since she never knew until the last minute whether her dad would be home to drive her to a party, there was no point in getting excited about going. How many times could she keep asking friends' parents for rides when her mother would never take a turn driving?

74

Agoraphobia

This business with her mother started when Allison's youngest brother was born, six years ago. Before that, her mom had taken her to piano lessons, to Brownie meetings, even up to the mall, where Allison got to push two-year-old Ben in the stroller. When she learned that her mom was expecting again, she liked the idea of a new baby in the family and hoped for a little sister. Allison had heard her parents arguing about the expense of a new baby and how the family would have to cut back on spending. It bothered her that Dad seemed to be staying away from home more. Even though her mom said he was working late to make extra money, sometimes Allison, in her room upstairs, heard him stumbling around drunk when he got home about midnight.

At first Allison went along with her mother's excuses for staying home after Joey was born. She knew how much energy and effort it took to get Joey and Ben freshly diapered, dressed, and into their infant and car seats. It was easier for Allison to ride her bike up to the store for things they needed before Dad got home. Six years later, though, Allison knew something must be wrong with a mother who never drove anywhere by herself and had excuses for every party or family get-together that came up.

If someone in your family seems like Allison's mother, she may be suffering from agoraphobia. I said "she" because many more women than men have this disorder. Although the word means "fear of the marketplace," agoraphobic people fear any number of situations. What these situations have in common is that someone who becomes extremely frightened believes she can't easily escape. Stores, buses, and theaters all hold the power to bring on panic.

Allison didn't know about an incident that happened shortly after Joey's birth. She was at school when her mother ran out of diapers unexpectedly and needed to go to the store. Her mom had not been out with the new baby yet, having left all the shopping to her husband. Still a little weak after childbirth, she nevertheless bundled up Joey and Ben, at that time three years old, and went to the store. She was so afraid Joey would start crying, or Ben would throw a tantrum if she didn't buy him something, that she began to panic. She grew dizzy, couldn't catch her breath, and felt her heart would burst from pounding. She managed to find a chair near the prescription pickup area and sat down until she felt better. Then she quickly paid for the diapers and went home, collapsing in tears on the couch. After that she began to pay close attention to all of her body's sensations, scared that she'd die of a heart attack and leave her three children without a mother. When she had a second panic attack on a routine grocery trip while her own mother was watching the two boys, she was convinced she was about to die. A visit to the doctor and some tests later that week revealed no apparent physical basis for her attacks.

Allison tried to be understanding with her mother. She knew her mother worried about her anytime she was away from the house, so she'd call home often. If she had to stay after school to work on a project or help a teacher, she'd always call, knowing her mother started watching for her as soon as school let out even though it was a fifteen-minute walk to their house. When her friends signed up for ski lessons after school, she didn't even ask if she could, too, knowing her mother would worry too much about her.

What really bothered Allison was the fighting between her mom and dad. She didn't blame Dad for getting upset. He could never go to parties or out for an evening with his wife, the way other men did. He always had to make some excuse for Mom. And the rare times he asked her, as a favor, to take care of an errand for him, she never came through. The sounds of their voices rising angrily late at night would drift down the hall to Allison's room, where she lay awake, afraid her parents would get a divorce. "If he leaves, it's all her fault," Allison thought, crying into her pillow.

Allison's father, too, was sympathetic at first. He made sure he got to the grocery store after work, and he tried to persuade his wife to go for short rides in the car while a baby-sitter stayed with the kids. He offered to baby-sit while his wife went out on her own or with friends, but she never took him up on his offers. Although he had blamed his wife for getting pregnant a third time when they couldn't afford it easily, he loved Joey, who was a good, easygoing baby. Still, he couldn't stand seeing his wife become a prisoner in their home.

As Allison's mother became more tied to the house, afraid that she might have a panic attack and faint or otherwise embarrass herself if she went out, her family lost patience with her. Although he shopped for groceries and other necessities for the family, Allison's father found more reasons to stay away from home. Slowly Allison's mother began to rely on her to take care of errands around the neighborhood. Although this made Allison feel important and grown up at first, she soon saw that her mother's fear of going out on her own was becoming a big inconvenience for her.

Other Anxiety Disorders

Agoraphobia is one of several problems called anxiety disorders. *Anxiety* is a psychological word for worry. All of us worry at times—about a test, getting a shot at the doctor's, going to a new school. Anxiety is considered a disorder—something needing treatment—only when it interferes with a person's activities and life in general.

Some anxiety disorders, called phobias, are limited in their effects, letting the person do most things with no problem. Many of us know someone with a fear of dogs or insects, for example. As long as she can avoid dogs or insects, everything's fine. We may tease the person for screaming at the sight of a spider, or go along with special arrangements, such as taking the long way around the block to stay away from a dog. In general, the person isn't handicapped in her daily life or seriously disturbing to her family.

Even phobias can become a problem to a family. Jerry's brother, Andy, had developed an intense fear of elevators after wandering into one and being separated from his mother at a large department store when he was four. When Andy was twelve, the family wanted to start taking vacations to a different big city each year, so that the boys could see the museums and other attractions. Although at home Andy was able to avoid elevators by using stairs or escalators, in New York City this would have been impossible. There was no point in going to New York if they couldn't visit the Empire State Building, World Trade Center, and other tall buildings.

The other anxiety disorders have different types of symptoms. Allison had a second cousin named Martha who could never leave the house without running back inside seven or eight times to make sure the stove was off. Anxiety that takes the form of repeated, unwanted thoughts or actions is called an obsessive-compulsive disorder. If someone tried to stop Martha from doing her checking, she became extremely fearful that something bad would happen. It seems that the unusual repetitive actions of obsessive-compulsive people keep their anxiety under control.

Other people with anxiety have a more generalized fear. Rather than being afraid of a specific object or situation, they feel tense and worried most of the time. Life itself is seen as dangerous. Any situation has the chance of showing the person's failures and weaknesses to everyone. Unfortunately, worry itself can interfere with the person's work and other activities, bringing on the failure that was feared to begin with!

Causes of Anxiety Disorders

Efforts to find the causes of agoraphobia and other anxiety disorders have focused on both physical causes, related to inborn traits in certain individuals, and important life experiences. We know now that, even as infants, we all have different ways of reacting to our surroundings. Some babies are calm and relaxed, crying only when they are hungry or wet. New people and unfamiliar situations don't seem to bother them. Other babies startle and cry at any little disruption to their normal routine. Whether conditions in the womb during pregnancy or traits handed down from parents are responsible, there seems to be little that parents can do to change this fearfulness drastically. With patience they may be able to lessen it, though.

Some researchers suggest that many people with agoraphobia were fearful as children, even in infancy. Other characteristics also show up often in the early lives of these people. Many had disrupted family relations—an alcoholic parent, a parent who died, or an unusual amount of responsibility, such

81

as helping an ill parent. Their actions were often criticized as not good enough. This may have made them feel guilty for disappointing others and afraid of openly expressing their opinions. What seems to happen under these conditions is that the person learns that staying away from difficulties leads to feelings of relief.

Allison's mother was only four when her parents divorced. She stayed with her mother, who remained bitter about her husband for the rest of her life. Allison's mother tried to avoid being seen as similar to her father by becoming responsible and "good." She never told her mother when she was angry, and she felt guilty any time school activities kept her from helping her mother at home. She took her desire to please and to avoid blame into her marriage. When she got pregnant with Joey, she worried constantly that her husband would leave her, as her father had left her mother. The stress of disagreements with her husband and fears that she couldn't handle three children combined to set off her panics. Only in the safety of her house could she relax from the added worry that she would panic in public and embarrass herself and her family.

The fear of having an anxiety or panic attack is very powerful. Agoraphobia can develop even in someone who has never had a panic attack, since just the fear of losing control or having a panic attack can keep someone in the house. However, if the person starts to experience any signs that panic is starting, this can help bring on the attack. Many agoraphobic people apparently become too tuned in to their body's reactions to stress or even physical activity. If worry or physical strain brings an increase in heart rate, dizziness, or other symptoms related to fear, they notice this right away and become alarmed. The person fears she will panic, and as a result avoids any scary situations. If escape or avoidance seems impossible, the fear can then escalate into panic.

People with obsessive-compulsive disorders seem to have a family history of depression, suggesting that the two disorders are related. The fear of failing terribly also seems to be involved in stirring up the repetitive thoughts and actions. When someone fears being less than perfect, perhaps as a result of parents' high expectations, it's hard for that person to relax and accept that mistakes can happen. Perhaps you can remember wanting to do something, or make a gift, for someone you cared about, and you wanted it to come out perfectly. You spent much more time on it than you normally would, no doubt, and you probably found yourself thinking about it at times when you were supposed to be

83

doing something else. This is a mild, brief example of a normal obsession and compulsion. For someone who is obsessive-compulsive, life itself can become an all day every day effort to make sure that things turn out perfectly.

The burden of an anxiety disorder limits the affected person's enjoyment of life and disrupts family relationships. Allison and her father became more and more angry at her mother for failing to participate in family activities. Because of Andy's elevator phobia, planning the family vacation became a search for locations without elevators. In Martha's family, every outing started out with arguments and frustration as the others waited in the car for Martha to finish her checking routine.

Treatment Methods

Fortunately there are many treatment methods that can be quite successful with anxiety disorders. However, as with other mental illnesses, gaining the person's participation can be difficult. One problem is that, for agoraphobics, merely leaving the house to go for treatment can be very difficult. Family members may need to reassure the person, maybe for months, that successful treatments are available before the person will leave the house. For someone with obsessive-compulsive disorder, efforts to stop the thoughts or actions, and even just the idea of stopping, can lead to so much anxiety that the person avoids the treatment. It's something like taking away the person's lucky charm. Much encouragement may be needed before treatment can start.

In trying to help people with anxiety disorders, mental health professionals often use a many-pronged approach. An important factor in helping the person with agoraphobia is educating her about her body's fear responses. If she understands what is happening when she climbs steps quickly or goes through a stressful situation, the person can avoid adding her own fearful thoughts to a normal and manageable experience.

Taking the knowledge a step further, people with agoraphobia also learn that a panic attack will go away and that they won't die from it. You probably realize that telling yourself "Getting a low grade on this test would be the worst thing in the world" will only increase your fear and lower your ability to concentrate on the test. In a similar way, when a person with agoraphobia says to herself, "I'm going to die," or "My heart is going to explode," her fear increases and the panic continues. Treatment may include training in using reassuring phrases such as "I can get through this OK" in stressful situations.

In many locations phobia clinics are now available for people with anxiety disorders. Allison's mother, with the urging of her husband and daughter, agreed to go to the program near their town. Gradually she learned about fear and began talking about the feelings of guilt, anger, and low self-confidence she had had when she was growing up. At the same time Allison and her father and brothers took part in family sessions. They learned how to help Mom face and overcome her fears. By knowing about and helping her through the phases of treatment, Allison became able to understand how her anger had only made her mother feel more of a failure. Allison's father could see how his staying away had made her more anxious and more depressed. Learning better ways of expressing their feelings and needs was helpful to all the family.

Finally, practice in going to places that were feared, starting with the easiest and gradually tackling more challenging ones, was an important part of the program. Allison found that helping her mother practice her outings and seeing her progress was much more fun than doing things for her. Watching her mother's growing skill at getting and staying relaxed, combined with her confidence that fear wouldn't kill her, was especially rewarding for Allison.

For people with simple phobias, outpatient treatment is generally brief. Usually relaxation techniques are taught so that the person can control his reactions while thinking about the feared object. The person gradually learns to stay relaxed while imagining more scary situations. Sometimes the therapist arranges practice outside the office with the feared object itself. When Andy's mother complained to their pediatrician about her son's phobia of elevators, she was told the name of a child psychologist. After five sessions of relaxing and imagining being in elevators, Andy was able to relax and ride in elevators with no further problems.

An interesting aid in learning relaxation is called biofeedback. While sitting in a comfortable chair, the person can watch colored lights or hear rising and falling tones, telling her how relaxed she's becoming. The electronic equipment that gives this "feedback" is constantly measuring the person's hand temperature, heart rate, or other signs of physical relaxation. Just as your teacher's comments and corrections help you know what you're doing right or wrong in math, the lights and sounds of the biofeedback machine help people know which of their thoughts and other responses are helping them relax.

When someone has obsessions or compulsions,

other approaches are needed. The person is encouraged to talk about past experiences that helped create the anxieties, and certain other techniques are used to help the person achieve control over the unwanted thoughts and actions. In severe cases, when the compulsion takes over the person's life, hospitalization may be needed. As with other serious disorders, there are both good and bad aspects of hospital treatment. The main benefits are that a complete evaluation of the person's health can be done, the person's response to medication can be observed, and protection against dangerous or unhealthy behavior is provided. But for most families, checking a family member into a hospital for treatment of a mental illness brings up many confusing feelings. Relief that the person is away and is getting treatment, guilt that perhaps they shouldn't be sending him there, and sadness at realizing and admitting the seriousness of the disorder are some common reactions of family members.

As in other mental illnesses, medications can be helpful in anxiety disorders. These include specific antianxiety drugs, antidepressant medications that often help with agoraphobia, and chemicals that lessen panic by lowering the body's response to fear. Some people with obsessions and compulsions have also responded well to medications. These medications can lessen the person's symptoms and make the anxiety more manageable, although they don't cure the disorder. They can also lift the depression that sometimes results from having a serious anxiety disorder, allowing the person to have more hope and energy. The person can then take part in the psychotherapy that will help her learn new ways to cope with stress. In many cases of anxiety disorders, psychological treatment has been successful without any medication.

Mental illnesses can be thought of as exaggerated forms of our normal reactions to stress. All of us have fears and worries at times. We may try to avoid what we fear, or use a special technique, like wearing a lucky shirt to an interview, to help us through. By reminding yourself of how you feel at stressful times, you can understand a bit of what a family member with an anxiety disorder is experiencing. This in turn can help you and your family member to get along better. You'll have more realistic expectations of what the anxious person can accomplish, and you'll understand why she has these problems. This can free you from trying to change the person, which may help the person feel more relaxed and less pressured. It's also a good idea for you to learn the same techniques of relaxing and coping with fearful situations and feelings that are part of the treatment of actual anxiety disorders. These techniques can help you deal with the normal challenges of life—parents, school, friends—in more effective ways than you may be using now. Since many people don't learn how to cope with self-doubts and other worries until they are much older, this will give you a valuable head start!

6

◆

Post-Traumatic Stress Disorder

Can you remember a time when you were so scared you started to shake, or got knots in your stomach? Perhaps the car you were in skidded suddenly on the ice. Or you were baby-sitting and heard a noise in the basement. Picture yourself in that situation as clearly as you can for a moment. Now pretend that whatever scared you that time happened every day for a year, and during that year you were far from all the people you know and care about. And imagine that, because of the fear, you did some things that, looking back, embarrass you, like throwing up or crying. Now multiply those feelings of fear and loneliness and shame by a thousand, and you can get a rough idea of what it was like to have been an American combat soldier in the Vietnam War. Many of those soldiers, plus nurses and others who helped in the war, make up the largest group of people suffering from an illness called post-traumatic stress disorder, PTSD for short.

What Is Post-Traumatic Stress Disorder?

Billy had trouble understanding why his father acted the way he did. At the age of fourteen, Billy thought of war as something they make you study in history. Of course, he heard bits of stories on the news about the United States sending weapons to faraway countries, but he never paid too much attention. And even though his brother Chuck had registered for the draft when he turned eighteen, Billy didn't worry about his brother or about his own turn to register in four years. People weren't being drafted now, anyway. But he knew that his dad's problems had something to do with his experiences in Vietnam.

Billy remembered when Dad lived with them, before Mom made him leave. Billy used to love it when Dad would play with him and Chuck, but it didn't happen often. Between working in the storeroom at the hospital and taking classes to become a heating technician, his dad didn't have a lot of time for playing.

The part Billy didn't like to remember was his dad's angry outbursts and the fights between his mom and dad. Billy and Chuck would peek around the corner of the stairway, watching to make sure their mom wasn't getting hurt, when Dad started throwing or punching things. It usually happened only after he'd been drinking, which he did most often in the spring each year. Billy and Chuck didn't know about their dad's terrifying nightmares. They also didn't know about the times when Dad was mentally back in Vietnam for a few seconds, reliving some secret terror. What they did know was that, unlike their friends, if they had G.I. Joe toys or pretended to shoot guns around Dad, he'd yell and send them to their room or even break the toys. After seven years of this, Mom got Dad to leave.

After the separation Billy's mom didn't want him and Chuck even to see Dad at first. She was scared that he'd get them all in a car accident while drinking. After a few months she started letting Dad come over to see the boys at their new apartment, while she'd find something to do in town. That way the boys could spend time alone with their dad. Eventually she let them go places with him and even stay over at his apartment, unless he was drinking. Billy knew that some of his friends whose parents were divorced never saw or heard from their fathers, so he was glad that his dad wanted to see him and Chuck. Still, even when his dad started dating first one woman, then another, he wished Dad and Mom would get back together.

By the time Billy was ten, his dad had seen two psychiatrists and one psychologist about his temper. Dad never told his doctors about his Vietnam experiences. Although the antianxiety medication he sometimes took helped a little, he still couldn't get through a year without a drinking bout. When he didn't take the medication, his temper was as bad as ever, causing his girlfriends to leave him, as Billy's mom had done. Somehow he was able to do his job without getting into any problems at work.

Finally, when Billy turned fourteen, his dad had some severe headaches and went for a complete checkup. The doctor asked him a lot of questions about how his life was going, not just about his health. At the end of the exam he suggested that Billy's dad go to some rap groups at the Veteran's Administration hospital. The doctor had treated other men who had served in Vietnam and had similar problems with drinking or drugs and violent behavior. Although Billy's dad was hesitant to bring up old memories, he figured that maybe he could get to the bottom of his problems once and for all. It took him six months to get up the nerve to go.

In her book *Home Before Morning,* Lynda Van Devanter described her personal journey from fun-loving nursing student, concerned about social issues, to veteran of Vietnam, torn apart by the gruesome and frustrating efforts to save lives and put together bodies. She told how, just before their Vietnam duty, she and a friend drove across the United States, sharing their thoughts and dreams along the way. They imagined themselves as world travelers, jetting from one glamorous spot to another, then switched gears and saw themselves as typical suburban housewives. Amazingly, in Long Island eight years later the same Lynda Van Devanter could drop to the floor and crawl on her stomach, in a sweat, from the bathroom to the living room after hearing a siren go off. Although she had been away from Vietnam for about seven years, Vietnam wasn't far away from her thoughts. Not until two years after that did she finally face up to what her experiences in the war had meant to her. Like Billy's father, she had to go through a lot of bad times before being convinced that she needed to confront the past.

Not all people with PTSD have been in combat situations. Dwayne used to like playing with his older brother, Kyle. All the times they shot baskets together and played catch had really helped Dwayne in his junior high sports. In Little League he wasn't afraid to pitch against anyone. Some of his friends told him they wished their brothers would spend time with them the way Kyle did with him. For the last year, though, Kyle hadn't seemed interested in anything fun. Ever since his accident he wanted to spend a lot of time in his room alone, just listening to the radio.

Kyle had been driving for about a year when he convinced his mom to let him drive with friends to a rock concert. They had a great time there, and on the way out they saw three girls they knew who needed a ride home. Even though the small car was already full, they didn't want the girls to have to wait for a bus in the dark. All seven teens piled in. They hadn't gone far when the car swerved and skidded into a tree. Kyle came to after the smash and saw blood on the dashboard and windows of the passenger side. Within seconds he heard sirens and saw two ambulances zoom up. Two of the girls were rushed to the hospital, where one of them died without ever coming out of a coma. Kyle had only a broken nose and bruises, but two of his friends needed physical therapy for their injuries. It turned out that something in the steering mechanism of the car wasn't quite right, and this, combined with the extra weight of so many passengers, had made the car go out of control.

Kyle's mother was upset about the injuries, the

girl's death, and the wrecked car, but she couldn't blame her son. After all, he had been trying to help out some friends. She and Dwayne worried about Kyle's reactions to the accident. He seemed jumpy all the time and had nightmares about the crash for months. Most upsetting was his change in attitude. He seemed to be turning from a friendly, popular boy into a loner.

Luckily the doctor recognized the signs of PTSD when Kyle's mother described her son's behavior. He recommended that Kyle receive ongoing counseling. Although Kyle's grades had dropped, he was still passing all his subjects, so the psychologist felt that no major damage had been done to Kyle's future plans for college. She could even write to the schools where Kyle hoped to go and account for the temporary drop in grades. Still, as she explained to Dwayne and his mother in a family session, Kyle's life had definitely changed. The goal was not for Kyle to forget the accident but for him to put it into perspective and get on with his life.

"Good Stress" and "Bad Stress"

These three examples—Billy's father, Lynda Van Devanter, and Dwayne's brother—show the effects of a special kind of stress. In order to understand stress, it's useful to think of situations that call for different, and more difficult, responses than our average, everyday activities. These situations are called stressors. In our feelings and thoughts, and in our bodies, we try to deal with the demands on us. Giving a speech in class, performing in a play, or taking over as quarterback in a big game can make us feel nervous, edgy, or afraid. Yet the tension we feel helps us concentrate and even perform better.

You have probably been aware of your own body's reactions to a stressor—the sweating, shaking, and blushing that go on at times like these. These reactions are the signs of our nervous system's activity under stress. Stress reactions can even happen at happy times, like a vacation or a holiday. Perhaps you've noticed how people in your family argue and snap at each other when they're getting ready for a big party or trip. In all of these situations, when the stressor is over, we get back to our old routines without any problem.

For most of us, the stress we face is normal. It's something everyone goes through at some time or other. Serious problems come up when a stressor is so overwhelming and frightening that we can't just put it behind us. Especially if our own or a family member's life is in danger, we're likely to react in ways that go beyond the ordinary. This is the special

98

stress that Billy's father, Lynda Van Devanter, and Kyle experienced.

Billy found it hard to accept that his father had PTSD. How could a person still be upset over something that happened fifteen years before? Dwayne had trouble understanding why Kyle hadn't bounced back to being his old self. They didn't know yet that intense stress or emotional trauma can damage a person, both physically and emotionally. The human body can prepare for "fight or flight," as the reaction to danger has sometimes been called, for only so long. Then high blood pressure and other physical symptoms can become long-lasting conditions. In a similar way, our mental attempts to cope with fear and guilt, for example telling ourselves "It wasn't my fault" or "It's no big deal," can hold up for only so long. The strong feelings can lead to depression, sleeplessness, and anxiety, or we may numb them with alcohol or drugs.

In post-traumatic stress disorder, the person's reactions to severe stress can show up in different ways, sometimes changing over time. Situations that remind the person of the stressor can be emotionally upsetting or bring back old memories to the point that the person is mentally "back there." Self-protection from additional fear and pain can take the form of feeling detached or emotionally numb, which interferes with relationships. Efforts to block out what happened can lead to avoidance of any possible reminders. Explosive anger and sleep problems reflect the person's oversensitivity to things going on around him.

Watching a parent relive a fierce battle can be a scary experience for children. Trying to be close to someone whose emotions are blocked off can lead to misunderstandings and hurt feelings. Tiptoeing around differences of opinion in order to avoid setting off an angry outburst can make family members tense and upset that their needs aren't being met.

Before his dad was able to talk about his experiences, Billy was angry at him for the violence that resulted in his divorce from Mom. Billy also worried that his dad would get killed after drinking, just as his mom had worried about Billy and Chuck when they were with Dad. And he was ashamed, when his teacher talked about the Vietnam War, that his dad had fought in it. Billy kept his feelings to himself most of the time, but he showed his anger indirectly. He avoided sports, knowing his dad would have loved for him to be on the school teams, and he spent his time listening to music, content to get C's and D's on his report card.

The change in Kyle left Dwayne with a lot of time

to himself. He missed being with his brother and worried that he had done something to make Kyle angry at him. He started taking out his frustration on kids at school, picking fights and acting tough.

Causes of PTSD

Unlike most of the disorders I've discussed, which have been known for many years, PTSD was first classified as a psychiatric disorder in 1980. The large numbers of Vietnam veterans who showed delayed and prolonged effects of their war experiences began to be noticed. Mental health professionals became aware that reactions to severe stress can last a long time. They may not even show up until years after the stress. Although in earlier wars terms like "battle fatigue" were used to describe the stress reactions that happened in combat, the idea of delayed reactions was new. As we learn more and more about the biology of our emotions, we are starting to understand how trauma can actually change our nervous systems. In this way, the effects of stress can persist over years.

Since wartime stress has long been known to bring on emotional reactions, you might wonder whether the Vietnam War was different in causing PTSD, and why. Billy's grandfather's experience is a good example of the difference between World War II and the Vietnam War. When Billy was growing up, he loved looking at Grampa's medals and old uniform and hearing stories about the war. His grandfather recalled the end of the war and how excited he and his friends were to learn they would be going home. On the troop ship back to the United States from Europe, they had time to talk about their experiences and start putting them into perspective. They were able to accept the fact that not all their actions had succeeded, but they knew their overall effort had been successful. When they got home, their families were proud of them, and their hometowns had parades and special events to welcome them. Grampa felt he had done a worthwhile thing in helping to defeat Hitler's army.

When Billy's father came home, he flew back to the United States with other soldiers, then flew on to his hometown alone. He left Vietnam, not after achieving a goal, but when his year's assignment was up. At the time he returned, the United States was still sending soldiers to Vietnam. Meanwhile college students and others all over the country were protesting American involvement in an Asian war. For Billy's father, there were no parades and no pride. No one outside his immediate family wanted to hear about his experiences, and he certainly didn't feel like telling them. He hoped that by avoiding all mention of the war he'd get over the dreams of bombs and killing, and the guilt of coming back in one piece, unlike some of his buddies. He wanted just to forget the whole thing. Unfortunately, he couldn't.

In a way, the adjustment of women who served in Vietnam was harder than that of the men, because there were fewer of them. They had fewer chances to come in contact with people who had shared similar experiences. Lynda Van Devanter wrote that people she met were completely surprised to find that women had been in combat areas. Even the organizers of the Vietnam Veterans of America group were shocked, when they met her, to learn she was a veteran. They had forgotten all about the women who had served in Vietnam. Luckily, she happened to be with her husband when he did an interview with the VVA organizers for his job. She mentioned her own experience as a Vietnam veteran. Otherwise, the needs of women veterans would have been ignored even longer.

Although we know clearly that situations of extreme danger and threat can cause PTSD, research is still under way to reveal why some people under those conditions develop PTSD and others do not. For example, do characteristics of the person before the trauma occurred affect how he will react? Kyle's father had left the family when the boys were young, and Kyle had tried to be the man of the house. The accident stirred up feelings of guilt and anger in Kyle as he saw his efforts to be responsible crumble. The authors of a study of Vietnam veterans have suggested that the meaning each soldier gave to his experience had an impact on his later adjustment. For Billy's father, killing enemy soldiers was an unavoidable part of war that he accepted. But seeing women and children killed, and not even knowing whose side they were on, did not fit into his idea of why he was over there.

Other studies have suggested that support from families and others can help lessen or avoid PTSD. Also, less severe trauma—greater distance from fighting, less risk of violent death—can result in less severe symptoms of PTSD.

Treatment of PTSD

As Billy's father did, many veterans received treatment for drinking and drug abuse, marital problems, and aggressive outbursts with no success. Opening up the old, buried memories and images of the war seems to be the necessary step for getting rid of the PTSD symptoms. Lynda Van Devanter described her one-on-one experience with a veterans' counselor, starting with a solid week of reviewing the details of her year in Vietnam. Putting the old fears and grief into perspective and creating a new understanding of her experience were only a beginning. With additional counseling, the emotional wounds would eventually heal.

Other Vietnam veterans have found it useful to talk about their experiences in groups with other vets, gaining the trust and confidence to discuss long-held secrets after hearing how others coped with their Vietnam past. We know from studies of victims of floods and other disasters that people need to talk about a catastrophic event over and over before they can fit it into the rest of their lives. Unfortunately, the unpopularity of the Vietnam War prevented many veterans from having this chance. Once they do take the opportunity to share and face their memories, they are able to take control over the fear, rather than letting the fear control them.

Medication can also be helpful in healing a "bruised" nervous system. Yet it's important to realize that medication will only serve as an emotional band-aid if the fear of bringing the trauma into the open remains. Billy's father's drinking could be understood as an attempt to numb himself against the

105

feelings of emptiness, guilt, and fear. This attempt brought only temporary relief. In addition, it brought him the anger and bitterness of his family.

PTSD is a kind of psychological grab bag resembling many other mental illnesses: anxiety, depression, psychosis-like hallucinations, and alcohol and drug abuse. What holds these symptoms together is severe, overwhelming stress, something that is not usually present in these other disorders. Understanding what your family member has been through and how the emotional reactions could last for years can help you and your family survive the ups and downs of PTSD.

When Billy's father began going to group sessions at the Veterans' Administration hospital, Billy was disappointed. This wasn't the magic pill he had hoped would take care of his dad's problems in one swallow. The time his father had usually spent with him, now that Chuck was in college, was going into veterans' activities. Billy hadn't expected this. Billy's father even began doing some peer counseling himself, to help other veterans start understanding the source of their problems. Then spring came along and he wasn't drinking, for the first time that Billy had ever known. After that, Billy was happy for any

106

time Dad spent on his involvement with the vets' group.

It's possible that bringing out all the old memories and re-examining them won't remove all the signs of PTSD. Sensitivity to certain sounds, such as sirens or helicopters, and occasional nightmares may persist. Still, these symptoms become much easier to handle when the whole traumatic event has been accepted and faced. It's as if the person says, for example, "I'm a father, a heating technician, and a poker player, and I spent a year in Vietnam," instead of "I'm a Vietnam veteran." The trauma is just one of many parts of the person's life. Controlling and accepting the fear instead of letting the fear control the person can make a big difference. It's even possible to go on to a satisfying and productive life following serious injury, which many people have done. The books listed in the References section include the stories of veterans who were disabled in the war and went on to find meaning and purpose in life.

Sadly, other victims of trauma become so overcome by depression that they are unable to turn their lives around. Friends and family may become disgusted with their efforts to block out the pain with drugs or alcohol or wild behavior. When this happens, all of the people who care about the person are left with the feelings of helplessness and lost hope that come with knowing that their efforts to help the person have failed.

Like any other serious mental illness, post-traumatic stress disorder may continue to bring problems to you and your family. Although big improvements are possible, there's no guarantee. Your job is not to find the right doctor or treatment for your ill family member, or to try to drag painful memories out into the open. Rather, your most important task is to understand what is happening and then concentrate on making the most of your own abilities and interests. By doing this, you can help to make your own life satisfying. Trauma victims can find strength and relief by facing the cause of their problems and fitting it into their lives. You, too, can be happier if you face the fact of your relative's illness and make a place for it among the other, more enjoyable parts of your life.

7

◆

Alzheimer's Disease

Ted sat in the waiting room, flipping through the latest copy of *People* magazine. Occasionally a sentence about a rock star's latest arrest or a movie actor's new role caught his attention, but most of the words in front of him didn't register. His parents were in the doctor's office, hearing the results of six months of tests and examinations on his grandfather. After the appointment, they'd take Ted to his cousin's house, then go out in the country to meet with an extended-care facility director. Even without a definite diagnosis, they all knew that Gramps would be needing more attention and care than the three of them could provide.

Ted remembered when his grandfather had his own house, back when Ted was in grade school. Some of his favorite activities were helping Gramps plant tomatoes in the spring, then weeding and watering the garden over the hot summer until finally the tiny green tomatoes appeared. Counting and sorting Gramps's collection of old campaign buttons was a fun way to practice long division, and later on the buttons were a help to Ted on his history tests, because they had familiarized him with the names of vice presidents that no one else had heard of.

It was hard for Ted to believe that the grandfather who now lived with them was the same man who used to fascinate him with explanations of everything from constellations to organic gardens. "Your father has a dementia of unknown origin," the doctor had told his mother when she brought Gramps for a checkup. "Dementia" meant the thinking problems Gramps had been having: difficulty remembering recent events, learning new information, finding the right words to express his thoughts, and concentrating. These problems could signal Alzheimer's disease. A complete physical, neurological, and psychological examination was needed.

At first Ted's family hoped that a treatable condition was causing Gramps's symptoms. Infections, nutritional imbalance, heart and lung diseases, a brain tumor or blood clot can cause temporary losses of mental abilities. If they are caught and treated, the person's memory can be restored. Depression might also make someone appear out of touch with reality and withdrawn. Even permanent damage, such as the kind that results from small strokes, would be better, Ted's family thought, than Alzheimer's disease, which has no cure and only gets worse with time.

The doctor asked Ted's mother to bring in all of the medications her father was taking so that he could look into their possible side effects in evaluating Gramps. Aging can change a person's response to medications. These medications could also be causing changes in thinking and memory.

The neurological studies and psychological tests helped the doctor know more exactly what kinds of problems Ted's grandfather was having in the areas of memory, problem solving, motor control, and sensing and making sense out of things that were going on around him. Recently developed procedures such as the CAT scan allowed the doctors a detailed look into Gramps's brain, adding to the information that would help determine the diagnosis.

The family members also were asked to describe the changes in Gramps's behavior that first made them suspicious that there was a problem. Whether the changes had occurred gradually or suddenly was important for the doctors to know in order to make the diagnosis. Early on, they recalled, he had shown occasional memory slips, asking "Where are my glasses?" or "Who are those new neighbors again?" He seemed less interested in going outside or trying new restaurants than he had been. In conversations he sometimes had trouble finding the right words for what he wanted to say. When this happened, he would get upset and go upstairs to his room. This stage had been going on for about a year.

As the symptoms progressed, Gramps had more and more difficulty doing tasks that required calculating and thinking. Going to the store, which meant having to make decisions and count money, got to be so upsetting that he started avoiding shopping trips. He seemed glued to his favorite chair, making up excuses for not going out. By this time other explanations for his behavior had been ruled out, and the diagnosis of Alzheimer's disease was made.

What Is Alzheimer's Disease?

You may remember when your family member with Alzheimer's disease was diagnosed, or perhaps you were too young to understand. Suspecting that someone you love has Alzheimer's disease is a very different experience from hearing a doctor say that he has it. Our own minds have ways of protecting us from truth that is too scary or awful. We tell ourselves that it won't turn out as we fear, and we try to ignore signs that point in that direction. After a health professional makes a diagnosis of Alzheimer's disease, it's hard to pretend that the dreaded words weren't spoken. Instead, we look for ways to prove that what we have just heard is not true. We may go from doctor to doctor, looking for someone who will tell us what we want to hear. We may ask the doctor for more tests, hoping that something was left out of the examination. After we finally accept that the diagnosis is correct, the feelings of sadness, anger, and hopelessness arise. Although Ted's family had tried to prepare themselves for the worst, hearing it was still a shock.

When Ted saw his parents come out of the doctor's office, he knew that what they had feared was true. All the color had drained out of his mother's face, and his father gently held her elbow, guiding her out of the waiting room. In the privacy of their car, Ted's mother just said over and over, "It can't be true. It can't be true." Ted felt shaky inside, not knowing what he should say to his mom or even what he felt. All he knew was that he didn't want

113

Gramps to turn out like the people in the TV show he had seen. Yet the changes he had seen in the last year and a half made him think that would happen.

By the time Ted got to high school, Gramps's thinking and memory losses had become more and more obvious. The football game he watched yesterday and the senator's name he heard on the newscast before dinner were quickly forgotten. Now Ted's parents were worried that Gramps was in danger of wandering from home and getting lost, of getting into a car and causing an accident, or of trying to cook something and starting a fire. They could lose their house and even their life's savings if Gramps accidentally hurt someone or damaged something.

Gramps was on the waiting list for a nursing home. In the meantime, even though they felt it was an expense they could have done without, they hired a practical nurse to stay with him in the daytime while no one else was home. This was the next best thing to having him in a place with around-the-clock supervision. Ted's mother could relax, knowing her father was being taken care of, although she was tired from working extra hours to pay for the help. She sometimes daydreamed about the vacations or nice things they could have had with all the money that they paid the nurse.

It was upsetting to Ted and his parents to see this man, who used to be pleasant and easygoing, fly into a rage if his pipe went out. It was even more upsetting when he sometimes had moments of clear thinking. Did this mean he would be fine after all? They felt as if someone were playing a mean joke on them. It hurt when Gramps became suspicious of Ted and his parents, accusing them of taking his money or belongings when he couldn't find them. This stage can be especially stressful for family members of Alzheimer's patients.

It took several years before Gramps began to need help with his toileting and bathing. By that time he was in the nursing home. Ted didn't even want to visit him, since Gramps didn't seem to know whether he was there or not. His mother still went once or twice a week to bring Gramps candy or anything else that might brighten up his day. Ted always knew when she had been there, since he'd come home from his classes to find her sitting and staring into space. He hated to admit it, but at times he wished Gramps would die. It bothered him to catch himself with these thoughts, and he didn't dare tell his mom about them.

The Stresses of Alzheimer's Disease

One of the difficulties of living with, or having, a close relative who has Alzheimer's disease comes in watching that person lose the ability to be a part of the family. Recognizing people, talking about new topics rather than old repeated ones, and recalling events of the past few weeks are things we all take for granted in the people we spend time with. Knowing that permanent brain changes are interfering with their relative's ordinary abilities affects family members in many different ways. The fact that Alzheimer's disease can progress slowly or fast, with unpredictable periods when symptoms level off, is confusing. It can make the family's efforts to adjust to what is happening or will happen that much harder.

Naturally, if someone close to you is suffering from this disease, you have experienced a lot of difficult feelings. It's common to feel angry at how unfair it is. Deep sadness at seeing the changes that are gradually occurring, with no chance of recovery, can come and go, keeping you up at night or distracting you from schoolwork. Fear and worry about how your parents will manage all the details and expense of caring for someone with Alzheimer's will also occupy your thoughts, especially if the waiting

116

period for a nursing home bed is months or years. If some of the responsibility for taking care of your relative has fallen on your shoulders, you may resent having to help out while your friends concentrate on classes, dating, and sports.

What's happening to your ill family member may be only one source of distress. Serious problems can arise in your family as a result of your parent or parents' having the main responsibility for caring for your relative. People of your parents' age are now being called "the sandwich generation." This means that they are sandwiched between two sets of people who need their help. Nowadays people are living longer because of new discoveries in medical science. This means that people like your parents don't have to care for only their children, who are getting close to independence. They must also care for their own parents, whose increasing age and disability are making them less independent. This comes at a time when your parents may be trying to save money for your college education or are perhaps looking forward to travel and other activities that they can enjoy when their kids are grown. The problem for you comes up when you need help with a project, or someone to take you to band practice, and Mom has to stay with Grandma so she doesn't wander off. Or Dad is crabby and irritable from the

117

stress of trying to find good care for your grand-mother. This leaves you with your feelings of sad-ness and frustration about Grandma and her worsening condition, plus your disappointment, hurt, and anger toward Mom or Dad.

For Ted, one bad part was not having Mom and Dad at his basketball games. He had looked forward for so long to playing basketball for his school, and he was really doing well. The nurse wasn't there in the evenings, so Mom and Dad had to take turns coming to the games. At least his friends' parents cheered him on.

Needless to say, your parents have plenty of anger and disappointment of their own at this point. If there are no aunts or uncles nearby who are able to share the responsibility, your parents may be espe-cially angry at having to do everything. Or suppose your mother hasn't had the best relationship with her parent. This can also create problems. The Alz-heimer's disease may mean an end to your mother's lifelong hope that someday she and her father would get along better, leaving her with guilt, anger, or even depression. Or your father may be stuck trying to help a parent who, he felt, never really was pleased with him. And because someone with Alzheimer's disease can live fifteen or twenty years with the disease, your parents may see just a long road of responsibility ahead with no relief in sight.

Alternatives in Care

What can be done to ease the stress in your family? Although putting an aging, ill relative into a nursing home is one alternative to home care, most grown-ups have trouble doing this without a lot of guilt feelings. "She took care of me when I was a kid; now she's sick and I'm abandoning her." Even if the nursing home idea is acceptable, finding a facility that seems good or comfortable for your relative may involve a long time on a waiting list before the person gets in.

Ted's mother knew that putting Gramps into a nursing home was the only possible way they could manage. They couldn't afford to have her quit her job and stay home with her father. Even if she did, she knew she couldn't take the stress of watching him day after day. Although she didn't love her job as a hairdresser, she looked forward to it just because it got her out of the house and away from her father and his problems. Still, her guilt feelings sometimes made her snap at Ted or his father without knowing why.

There are alternatives to nursing homes, at least

119

for Alzheimer's patients in the early stages. Day treatment programs may be available at hospitals in your area, offering social activities and medical care for several hours a day. Sometimes a foster home situation can be used. This means that your elderly relative would live with a foster family who is paid by the state to care for the elderly. If your parents are at work all day and no one is home with your relative, this arrangement might be better than care in your home. For people in the most advanced stages of Alzheimer's, though, there may be no possibility besides some type of nursing home or hospital.

Some local support groups for families of Alzheimer's patients offer respite care. Families can arrange for someone to watch their family member while they take a vacation or other break from full-time care. Having these occasional breaks to look forward to can really help when you're living with someone who has Alzheimer's disease. However, not all families feel comfortable leaving their confused relative with a stranger, even for short, infrequent periods.

If your family decides to try home care, certain changes in your house may be necessary. In Ted's home, support handles in the bathtub, better lights in the hallway, and different door locks were helpful in keeping Gramps safe without being too inconvenient to Ted and his parents.

Treatments for Alzheimer's Disease

Although Alzheimer's disease has no cure, your relative must still take medications for other conditions that are common in older people. These other problems should not be ignored just because an elderly person has Alzheimer's. Whatever medications your family member needs, it's important for your family to keep careful track of what he should take and when, since he will not be able to do this for himself. Helping to give the right dose of medication at the right time may be one way that you have been involved in your relative's care. Watching out for side effects and telling the doctor if they occur also are important jobs for you and your family.

Scientists have tried to find chemicals that slow the progress of the disease or reduce the memory loss. Unfortunately, these medications have proven to be only slightly helpful so far and have been used mainly in research studies. Other, nonmedicine types of therapy are sometimes useful with Alzheimer's disease patients. Psychotherapy can help the person in the early stage deal with depression,

121

so that he doesn't waste valuable weeks or months, even years, when he can still take part in family activities. Getting a diagnosis of Alzheimer's disease is naturally a shock to the person, as well as to family members, and depression can affect everyone involved. Becoming depressed only adds to the family's problems and doesn't take into account the fact that no one knows how quickly the disease will get worse. If family members can be helped to overcome depression and get on with making the most of their relative's abilities, this is helpful to everyone.

The doctor who evaluated Ted's grandfather suggested that the family see a family therapist that he knew. At first Ted's mother ignored this idea, feeling that she could handle her emotional reactions and that Gramps wouldn't go. When she found herself spending more and more time on weekends just sleeping, she decided that a few sessions couldn't hurt and might even help. Although Gramps seemed to have up and down moments whether he went or not, Ted's mother found it helpful to talk about her worries. Talking about things out in the open made Ted feel that he was an important part of the family and gave him a chance to get answers to his questions.

Since no one can predict how quickly a particular

person's disease will progress, it is important for you and your family members to give your relative as much caring attention as you can. Just as cancer is no longer automatically hopeless in most cases, a diagnosis of Alzheimer's disease may not mean that your relative will quickly sink into complete helplessness. Encouraging him to do what he's able to do, and sharing an interest in him, will do more good than waiting for the worst to happen.

Reality orientation is a program, used in some hospitals and nursing homes, that focuses on getting patients to say and pay attention to what day of the week it is and other things they should know in their daily life. Although not everyone agrees that this works, it can certainly be helpful in keeping patients active and involved with other people. Participating in reality therapy sessions is much better than being alone and apart from people and activities.

Causes of Alzheimer's Disease

As with many disorders of the brain, our knowledge of what causes Alzheimer's disease is far from complete. We know that certain parts of the brain are damaged in specific ways. What produces these changes is still under study. As in other mental illnesses, there does seem to be an association within families, meaning that those with Alzheimer's disease usually have several relatives who also have or had it. What makes the disease occur in families in this way is not yet known. Studies of viruses of the nervous system, and of excess aluminum in brain cells of some Alzheimer's disease patients, have pointed to two possible causes. Whether, and how, these substances might be involved in causing the brain damage of Alzheimer's disease is not yet clear. The main thing that is known at this point is that as people get older, their chances of getting Alzheimer's disease increase. Researchers have yet to learn how aging allows these changes to take place in the brain and why only some elderly people develop this disease.

Until quite recently, being senile (feebleminded, forgetful) was thought to be a normal part of aging. Yet many famous (like George Burns) and not-so-famous people continue to be busy and productive late in life without losing their mental powers. If people just assume that being senile is an unavoidable part of growing old, they may ignore forms of memory loss that can be treated. Every elderly person who shows signs of memory loss and confusion deserves to be evaluated thoroughly.

The Alzheimer's Disease and Related Disorders

Association is an important support and information group for families affected by these problems. If you and your family have not joined this organization, I hope you'll look up the address at the end of this book and write to them. Once again, knowing all you can about the disease and getting to know other people who are dealing with it in their families is the best thing you can do for yourself.

8

◆

Eating Disorders

November 25

My first time home from college! It seems so strange to be back with my parents and sister. I guess I can put up with Dad's rules for the next few days. I can't believe how good Beth looks. She's finally trying to lose weight. I guess getting on the cheerleading squad gave her the push she needed . . .

December 20

I made it through exams! Now I just hope I got a 3.5 average. Dad will spaz out if I got anything less. Mom says she'll be happy with a 2.75—at least someone realizes how much time pledging a fraternity can take. Beth looks fantastic. I really think she's starting to overdo it, though. She eats a tiny salad every night and just pushes the other food around. I think she noticed me watching her 'cause she pretended to eat, but hardly anything left her plate. Mom and Dad are so proud of her, I don't know how they don't notice that even her new clothes are starting to hang on her.

December 26

I'm starting to worry about Beth. I heard her vomiting last night after the Christmas party. I knew she was eating more than her usual amount since her diet. She swore to me that she never made herself throw up before but she felt uncomfortable from all that food. She promised she won't do it again. I told her she'd better not, or I'll tell Mom and Dad about what she did this time.

January 2

I had a long talk with Beth. She realizes now, I think, that losing any more weight would be dumb and that she should just eat normally. I hope she can do it. She's a great kid, artistic, athletic, and a good student too.

March 20

I feel sick. Even though Mom warned me about Beth, I wasn't prepared for the shock of seeing her. She looks like a skeleton! Not only that, she acts like a different person. She used to laugh and joke around; now she's so serious all the time. It seems like all she does is study, exercise, and play with her food. She also wants to mess around in the kitchen making food for *other* people! She and Dad are in a battle of wits and wills, it seems. He tells her what to eat and weighs her, and she finds ways to trick him about what's going on. I told Mom to get her to a doctor, but she wants to give Dad's plan a chance to work. They're dreaming. There's no way Beth will let him win.

The Types of Eating Disorders

Although Beth's brother Mark wasn't an expert on anorexia nervosa, he could see the signs of a serious problem. Anorexia nervosa and the other main eating disorder, bulimia, have become better understood in the last twenty years than they were in the past. Unfortunately, the number of cases of these disorders has been growing, especially among girls and women.

Like Beth, anorexics are often successful, happy people, at least in the eyes of others. Yet, as Beth saw things, she was never quite good enough to be sure of herself. There was always the chance of messing up on the next test or not being accepted into the next art show. When she started to lose weight, though, she found that this was one thing that she could do perfectly. This was also one area of her life that she could control completely. As the compliments piled up, she feared that she might gain the weight back, disappointing her friends and family and herself. Why not lose another five pounds just to be on the safe side? Soon she was counting calories like a pro, calculating the value of everything that touched her lips. If she ate anything extra, she made sure she ran an additional two miles to take care of it.

Mark was angry at first that Beth had lied to him. How could he help her if she was shutting him out? He had always helped her before. When she broke her leg in sixth grade, he brought home all her homework from school and helped her keep to a schedule for getting it done. She had helped him, too, giving him ideas on what to get his various girlfriends for their birthdays. And yet, here she was, twenty pounds under her healthy weight, after telling him she wouldn't keep trying to lose weight.

Watching her during spring break, Mark began to realize that she wasn't happy after losing all that weight. She seemed to be frowning all the time. It made him sad to think she was so unhappy with her life that she was almost starving herself to death.

129

Mom and Dad were another story. Dad acted like a prison warden, watching over Beth's meals, while Mom tried to act as though everyone was getting along perfectly. Mark knew one thing for sure. Unless things improved, he'd have to find a summer job in another city, because there was no way he'd last through the summer with the three of them. He felt guilty about trying to get away from the situation, but he didn't think he could stand watching his sister either keep lying and win, or crumble under their dad's rule. If only it hadn't started after he left for college. Maybe it was all his fault for leaving!

Back at school after spring break, Mark learned to make his weekly calls home when Beth was usually out running. That way he could find out from his parents what was going on. If Beth happened to be home when he called, he would talk about safe topics of conversation.

Mark was relieved when he learned that his parents had taken Beth for a complete physical. Still, he wasn't relieved to hear what damage she had been doing to herself with her dieting. Her periods had stopped, her digestive system was a mess, and her hair and skin were in terrible shape. The pediatrician recognized that Beth had anorexia nervosa and referred the family to a psychologist. At least things were moving in the right direction.

What makes these eating disorders especially difficult for families is the lying and hiding that goes on. When someone is in a depression or has an anxiety disorder, it's obvious to the people around him. The person who's feeling miserable is focused on himself and doesn't think about hiding his condition. The person with an eating disorder, however, tends to become sneaky. She avoids the big scenes at mealtimes, for example, by eating alone, after making excuses for not eating with the family. The goal of being thin becomes the most important thing in the person's life. Comments by others are misinterpreted. "Shouldn't you eat a little more, dear?" is thought to mean, "You need to fatten up." Or "You're starting to look much better" is misunderstood as "You're getting heavy again." Under these conditions, family and friends are seen as enemies standing in the path of the person's goal of being thin.

In her book *Starving For Attention,* Cherry Boone O'Neill described her successful attempts to fool the people that cared about her. Even while staying in the hospital, she figured out tricks to make people think she was gaining weight.

In spite of all the security I managed to persist in my inane behavior. For example, meal breaks were required for my nurses. When they went to the cafeteria for twenty minutes, I took advantage of their absence by vigorously exercising. In the secluded therapy bath I did leg lifts. But the most incredible obstinance of all was my habitual showering or teeth brushing, which strategically followed each meal. With the door closed and water running I proceeded to vomit my carefully prepared meals. I was never apprehended in my games.

Although there is some overlap between the two, people with eating disorders are usually thought to fall into two groups, those with anorexia nervosa and those with bulimia. Anorexics severely cut down on their food intake while they exercise almost compulsively. It's not surprising that this combination leads to major weight loss. This self-starvation is damaging to the body and carries the definite risk of death. Bulimics maintain their weight close to the normal range, but they achieve this through "binge eating" and "purging." Although the person with bulimia might eat fairly normally during the day, at night she will eat huge amounts of food (binge). Eating so much makes her afraid of gaining weight, so she then forces herself to vomit or takes a large quantity of laxatives (purges), or both. The word *bulimarexia* is sometimes used to refer to those people who both lose large amounts of weight *and* use bingeing and purging to achieve their goals.

In both of these disorders, the body's normal signals of hunger and fullness become distorted. Beth's father suggested that she concentrate on eating when she was hungry and stopping when she was full, but there was no way for her to do this. What sounded so simple had become an impossibility. Even if she could have done it, she would have become so worried about overeating and losing all control over her weight and appearance that she would have found some way to work off what she had eaten.

Causes of Eating Disorders

The large increase in the number of people with eating disorders over the last twenty years has often been blamed on our society's emphasis on thinness, especially for girls and woman. In fact, eating disorders do occur most often in teenage girls and young women. In TV shows, commercials, and movies, a slender figure is shown to be the key to happiness and success. Since not everyone who observes these examples develops an eating disorder, however, other causes must enter into the explanation.

Research on those causes has focused much attention on family relationships of anorexics. There seems to be some agreement that families with an anorexic member tend to be close-knit, to the extent that people within the family are overly involved with one another's decisions and activities. In addition, parents in these families seem to try too hard to protect their children and to avoid open discussions of anger and disagreements.

Because bulimia has only been recognized as a separate disorder fairly recently, fewer studies have been done on its causes. Information that is available so far suggests that the families of bulimics have more conflict and arguments and less closeness and affection than families with an anorexic person. Families of people with bulimia seem also to have more cases of alcoholism and obesity, as well as depression, than families with someone who is anorexic.

Studies have revealed that eating disorders are more common in families of anorexic or bulimic individuals than in families of people without eating disorders. Again, how this influence is passed from one family member to others is not clear. It's important, however, to remember that not all relatives of people with eating disorders develop eating disorders themselves.

One cluster of traits that shows up in people with anorexia is a wish to be perfect along with fears of growing up and becoming independent from the family. In fact, this group of characteristics seems to separate people with eating disorders from "normal" dieters who want to be thin and fear being fat. In Beth's case, wanting to be a cheerleader was just one more step in her march toward being the best in every aspect of school. From her earliest years her parents' efforts to encourage her many talents gave her the idea that unless she was the best, they would be disappointed in her. At the same time she felt that without their guidance she could never succeed on her own.

For Cherry O'Neill, growing up at the height of her father Pat Boone's success as a popular singer was fun and exciting. Yet Hollywood held up a distorting mirror in which any imperfection threatened to end the family's and her own dream world of success. Combined with her father's strict rules and her closeness with her mother, this gave her the ingredients for developing an eating disorder. Somehow her three sisters found other ways of coping with the pressures of being in a performing family, reminding us how hard it is to pinpoint why any particular person develops a particular mental illness.

Wendy's bulimia developed after she lost weight at age fourteen. Her family life had little of the rosy glow that Beth's and Cherry O'Neill's families appeared to have from the outside. Her parents' marriage had been rocky for years, but for some reason they stayed together. Her two older brothers never had much time for her, leaving her jealous of friends who had close relationships with their brothers or sisters. Her mother, seemingly stuck in an unhappy marriage, was depressed for long periods of time. Wendy could understand why, since her parents evidently did everything they could to annoy each other.

When Wendy lost sixteen pounds, her brothers and their friends suddenly seemed to notice her. Afraid that they might go back to ignoring her, she developed a diet that seemed to guarantee success in keeping the weight off. By eating no breakfast and only an apple for lunch, she could eat a normal supper without gaining weight. Yet, on rare occasions at first and then more often, the hours between supper and bedtime became her downfall. Worried about a test or unhappy with her friends, she would distract herself by eating. Hating herself for "pigging out" late at night on every high-calorie food in the house, she tried to undo the damage by forcing herself to vomit. When she found herself starting to think about using laxatives to further control her weight, she knew it was time to get help.

Treatment for Eating Disorders

Treatment for eating disorders usually involves two main efforts, physical and emotional. The person must get back to a healthy weight and healthy eating habits, and she must also deal with the psychological problems at the root of the disorder. For anorexics, hospital treatment may be necessary. Some refuse treatment until their weight is so low they are on the verge of death. Or they become dangerously dehydrated through abuse of laxatives and diuretics. If they are in a weakened condition, they may accept food without a fight until they show a slow but steady weight gain. If they are strong enough that death is not a danger, however, they will probably resist any efforts to force a weight gain. In some hospitals patients must earn their exercise and activity privileges by showing a certain minimum weight gain each day. This encourages their cooperation in eating.

Cherry O'Neill's two weeks in the hospital were wasted because of her own nonstop efforts to fool the doctors and her family about her food intake. It was only later, when she and her husband moved to a different state and began marriage counseling on an outpatient basis, that she began to face up to her actions. With the help and support of her husband and friends, she was gradually able to find better ways to cope with her fears and worries. Even so, progress was often followed by setbacks before she overcame her disorder.

Whether in the hospital or on an outpatient basis, psychotherapy is necessary in treatment of anorexia. In part, this involves education, or helping the person to understand how her thought processes must change in order for her to become healthy. Learning to face and deal with disagreements with family members and to accept that everyone makes mistakes are also important ingredients. Finding ways to like herself is essential.

Antidepressants also have helped people with eating disorders. Exactly why this happens is not yet known. Perhaps these people are depressed and the medication lifts the depression, or it may be that the medication has a direct impact on the eating disorder.

Beth's hospital stay was only four weeks, while her weight got up to a safe level. During her inpatient treatment her parents came to the hospital to participate with her in family therapy sessions. These sessions helped her and her parents find better ways of dealing with their disagreements than ignoring them. When Mark came home for the summer, he also took part in some sessions. He learned how to be helpful to Beth in ways that she wanted and not just according to his own ideas. Beth's parents realized that they couldn't force Beth to eat and that it was up to her. Beth also started working on developing a separate identity for herself apart from her parents' expectations. The sessions continued when she left the hospital. As Beth approached a desirable weight, she joined a support organization for anorexics, which had a newsletter that she found helpful.

Treatment of bulimics is usually done on an outpatient basis because their weight loss isn't at a dangerous level. Although each mental health professional may have his or her own program, the main features of treatment are similar in many ways to the psychological treatment of anorexia. The bulimic patient must come to understand that both her striving for a perfect body and her focus on her weight are taking the place of other feelings of distress and dissatisfaction with herself. She also learns that her bingeing is a way of distracting herself from problems and sad feelings. Finally she finds more enjoyable and useful ways of coping with these feelings, which can then take the place of the focus on thinness.

It often seems that symptoms of a mental illness can serve an important purpose. Staying in the house relieves the agoraphobic person's fear that a panic attack will occur, and compulsions lessen the obsessive-compulsive person's fear of making a mistake. The eating disorders also appear to serve a purpose. All of us dislike certain things about ourselves or our lives. The person with an eating disorder trades the frustration of feeling unable to change what she doesn't like for the illusion of perfect control—over her weight.

As a family member observing this struggle, your natural reaction may be to tell the ill person how to solve her problem. What's hard for families to learn, and what family therapy can teach them, is that the person must take charge of her own progress at some point. Backing off can be the first step in truly helping your family member.

140

9

◆

Who Can Help?
Mental Health Professionals
and What They Do

Mark felt uneasy as the hospital elevator climbed slowly to the sixth floor. Part of him was glad that his sister was in a place where people could make sure that she was eating right. He also was hopeful that group therapy and other programs in the hospital would help Beth have a better feeling about herself. Still, he couldn't help being disappointed that Beth hadn't been able to make progress in her outpatient psychotherapy. A hundred questions rushed through his mind as the elevator jerked to a stop: "How will she react to me now? Will she blame me for her being in the hospital? What does she do here all day?"

Perhaps you, too, have wondered about your ill relative's treatment. You may have been curious about all these people who were becoming involved in your relative's life and your own, whether these mental health people were working in a hospital setting or in an outpatient office. Although someone in a white coat may seem scary or distant at first, getting to know the people who are caring for your family member can be useful. That way, when you have questions about what is likely to happen in the future or how you can help, you'll have someone to ask.

Adolescent Psychiatry—Turn Left at End of Hall, announced the white sign with large red letters. Mark could see some teenagers sitting and talking in the reception area. He showed his hospital visitor's pass at the desk and entered the adolescent unit. Beth's room, 627, was empty, but he recognized her stuffed animals on one of the beds. "Hi, I'm Maria. Who are you looking for?" a young nurse asked him. When he told her Beth's name, she smiled and said, "Oh, I'm her psych nurse. She's probably in art therapy now. She'll be back in five minutes. Why don't you just sit here and wait for her?" Mark felt some relief to know that this pleasant, confident-looking young woman was there for his sister to talk to.

When Beth came in, Mark's first impression was that she had gained a little weight since the last time he had seen her. "So you found my cell," she joked, and they hugged. Then Beth offered to show Mark around. He gladly took her up on it, figuring that way he wouldn't have to decide what he should and shouldn't try to talk about. After all, she had gotten pretty upset with him the times he had tried to give her advice on her eating problem.

As Mark and Beth walked to the lounge, Beth said hi or waved to other patients and staff members. It seemed to Mark that she had somehow adjusted to this place. Would she be able to give up the security she had here when she was at a safe enough weight to leave the hospital?

Activities Therapists

The lounge was a large room with a TV, couches and soft chairs, tables for card games, and lots of windows. "This is where I go a lot when I'm not in a scheduled activity," Beth said. The room reminded Mark of the lounge in his dorm at college, except that some of the teenagers here were as young as thirteen.

Next to the lounge was the art therapy room, where Mark met the two art therapists. One was a middle-aged woman named Mildred, whose paintings were in art shows all around the city. The other was a young woman named Kathy, who recently had graduated from an art therapy program at the small college nearby. They both seemed impressed with the pottery Beth was working on.

Mildred explained to Mark that most of the patients loved art therapy, even the ones who never liked art in school. Some patients expressed their feelings through their work, pounding on clay or splattering paint on paper. Others got a feeling of peacefulness, or control over themselves, as they carefully moved from an idea to a finished product. They also enjoyed the companionship, as groups of three or four patients, with one of the art therapists, talked about all kinds of things during the hour.

Working as art therapists gave Mildred and Kathy a chance to use their artistic talent while helping people make their lives better. Mildred had been an artist for many years, painting at home while her children were small. As her children got more independent, she wanted to do more than paint, so she took classes to become an art therapist. Kathy had volunteered in hospitals since she was sixteen and knew from her first day at college that she wanted to study art therapy. When an opening in the adolescent psychiatry unit came up after she graduated, she grabbed the chance.

Art therapy is often among the activities therapies available in a mental health treatment program. Music therapists use music and dance to help patients express their feelings. Recreation therapists lead sports and group activities to help people develop or improve social skills. Although you may not meet the people who work with your family member in these activities, it's good to know that these therapies aren't just "busy work." They give structure and purpose to the person's days in the hospital, they help the person learn to communicate and develop self-esteem, and they can help someone learn new interests and skills that can be continued outside the hospital.

Psychiatric Nurses

At the nurses' station Beth introduced Mark to some of the nurses. It seemed like a hubbub of activity there, with people writing in charts, conferring with doctors, putting medications into little cups to take around to patients, and talking on the phone. Maria, the nurse Mark had first met, asked if Beth wanted her to talk to Mark. Beth said they could all three talk if her roommate was out of the room.

They went back to Beth's empty room, and Maria asked Mark how Beth seemed to him. He described his reactions to seeing her, and Maria told him that Beth had really been working hard. She showed

145

Mark the weight and activity charts on the wall, where Beth's weight gains were recorded each day and her earned activity was checked off. Maria explained that, as a psychiatric nurse, she wasn't Beth's main therapist. She was there to help her when she felt discouraged and to listen as Beth tried to figure out her fears about her weight and appearance. She took part in weekly case reviews, where doctors or other staff went over each patient's progress, so she knew where Beth needed to focus her energies. When Beth complained that her roommate was playing the radio too loud, or got upset when a pair of pants felt too tight, Maria would remind her of ways to cope with these challenges. Maria would write any important information in Beth's chart so that the nurses on the next shift would know what was happening. In Mark's experience, nurses were people who gave shots, drew blood, or changed bandages, so hearing what Maria did gave him a new outlook on nurses.

Psychiatric Social Workers

Maria left to see another of her patients, and Mark and Beth went over to a different hallway. They stopped at a closed door with a sign that said Jack Fisk. Beth listened at the door, then knocked. "This is my group therapist," Beth explained, as they heard a voice tell them to come in. "We all use first names in group," Beth added.

From the diplomas and certificates on the office wall, Mark could see that Jack was a master's degree social worker. That meant that he had taken two years of courses and supervised work experience in social work after he graduated from college.

Jack told Mark that each patient had two group therapy sessions a week. Beth's group had six other patients, all with different types of emotional problems. Jack said that his favorite thing about running a therapy group was that, even with their different symptoms and problems, the patients always found they had certain important things in common. In particular, they usually had a low opinion of themselves and were afraid to be open about their feelings with other people. It really helped when they realized they were not the only people in the world who felt that way.

Jack talked a little about the other activities keeping him busy. Besides Beth's group, he also had a group for married couples. Husbands or wives of hospital patients would come in one evening a week to talk about marriage problems. He also saw some patients once a week for psychotherapy after they left the hospital. Beth wasn't sure whether she

147

would continue her therapy "work," as they called it, with Jack after she left, with Dr. Frank, her psychiatrist, or with her psychologist, Dr. Michael.

Clinical Psychologists

After Beth's pediatrician had decided she probably had anorexia nervosa, Beth's parents were given the names of several psychologists. They decided on Dr. Elaine Michael after talking with each one on the phone. Like the other psychologists, Dr. Michael had finished college, then had gone to graduate school, where she studied psychology for four years. She had also spent a year working in a hospital on a mental health unit, where she gave psychological tests, conducted evaluations of new patients, and did psychotherapy. After earning her Ph.D. degree and leaving the hospital, she decided she wanted to have her own private practice. It took a while to become known in the community, but now she was busy, treating several types of patients.

Although Beth had liked Dr. Michael from their first meeting, she had had trouble trusting her right away. After all, she hadn't trusted her family members for years. She kept a lot of things to herself, including her continued attempts to lose weight. When she lost another four pounds, Dr. Michael

148

told her parents that inpatient treatment was necessary.

One thing that had upset Beth about going into the hospital was that she couldn't continue to see Dr. Michael. Since no psychologists in private practice were on the staff of the hospital, Dr. Michael could only visit Beth sometimes. She couldn't participate in her treatment. In most states psychologists or social workers who see people for outpatient psychotherapy can't continue to treat them if they go into the hospital. Starting over with another mental health professional can disrupt the person's treatment. Yet if everybody with a mental illness tried to go to a psychiatrist on the staff of a hospital, there wouldn't be enough psychiatrists to take care of them all. This is one of the problems of the mental health system. Fortunately, lawmakers in some states are trying to correct this situation.

Psychiatrists

When Beth was admitted to the hospital, Dr. Frank became her doctor. Dr. Frank was a psychiatrist who had been working with children and teenagers for twelve years. He had graduated from medical school and then trained at a hospital for five years to become first a psychiatrist and then a child

149

psychiatrist. He hadn't always planned to be a child psychiatrist. During his medical school years and in his first year of residency training at a hospital, he had some experience with people who were mentally ill. He decided that he enjoyed talking to people about their problems for a half-hour or an hour, more than he liked seeing patients with physical problems for ten or fifteen minutes at a time. He liked getting to know the patients and their families. He also was pleased when some patients showed big improvements in their symptoms after they started taking medication. Since family members often found it hard to know how to act toward their relative, it was important for the whole family to find ways of communicating with one another. Were they trying to "baby" the person? Did they expect too much progress too soon? These were some of the issues he dealt with in family therapy sessions.

Beth had seen Dr. Frank that morning before Mark came, so Mark didn't meet him. Later that week a family therapy session was scheduled, so Mark would meet him then. Mark hoped that the therapy Beth and the family were getting would make life at home a little less tense during summer vacation than it had been at spring break.

Beth and Mark went back to her room. Her roommate, Diana, was there this time. Diana also was

150

sixteen. She had been admitted to the hospital for severe depression the week before. Her parents were divorced, and for the past year she had been living with her father and his second wife. Diana hated her stepmother and felt that her father and stepmother wished she would disappear. When her brother found a note she had written to a friend saying she sometimes wanted to die, her father had her hospitalized.

Diana asked Mark and Beth if they wanted her to leave, but Mark was getting ready to go home. He couldn't help wondering what an attractive girl like Diana was doing in a psychiatric unit of a hospital. Then he realized, anyone might also wonder that about Beth! Having seen the other patients and Diana, Mark was starting to understand that "mental patients" don't carry a sign or wear a tattoo that says Mentally Ill. Anyone could have a mental illness, and you wouldn't know it by looking at him.

Whether your own relative has been in a hospital or not, you may have come in contact with some of the types of mental health professionals Mark encountered. Perhaps your family is in a prepaid health program or health maintenance organization, where all the doctors and other staff work for the same company. Or your family may be using the services of a community mental health center. Regardless of the type of health care program you are using, the kinds of staff members who are involved with your family probably work in one of the mental health fields I've discussed.

Before you let yourself get frightened of your family member's therapist because you've never talked to a psychiatrist or psychologist or social worker before, remember one thing. They're people, too. As with any adults you meet—teachers, dentists, optometrists—there will be some you like and feel comfortable with, and others that you don't like. It's good to keep in mind that people who go into the mental health field do so because they want to help others. And if helping your ill family member means answering your questions, that's part of the job. Keep in mind that you might not get to hear details of your family member's illness because of confidentiality rules. Still, any other reasonable questions are fair game. You might even find yourself discovering a whole new career to consider!

10

◆

How You Can Cope

There are both helpful and hurtful ways of coping with the strong feelings that come from having a mentally ill family member. The hurtful ways—using drugs or alcohol, letting grades drop, fighting, to name a few—can't solve the problem and make you feel worse. In this chapter, I'd like to explain in more detail how you can find helpful ways to deal with your situation. It would be a good idea for you to have some paper and a pencil nearby.

Asking for What You Need

Barbara's older brother, Brad, had schizophrenia. Occasionally he stopped taking his medication, resulting in relapses of his schizophrenic symptoms. When this happened, their mother would drop everything to get him back into treatment, leaving

153

Barbara to take care of her younger sister, Carrie. It had gotten to the point where Barbara pulled away from her friends and stopped making plans with them, afraid that a return of Brad's symptoms would come up and ruin everything. By cutting herself off from friends, Barbara ignored an important part of her life. Social activities help prepare teens to be adults who can get along with a variety of people. Missing out on this, Barbara became lonely and depressed.

Barbara's best friend encouraged her to sit down and talk about this problem with her mother. Barbara waited for a time when things were pretty calm at home and her mom wasn't real tired. Barbara's mother had noticed that Barbara was staying home a lot more, but she hadn't really wondered about it. With Brad's illness and the cost of his treatment on her mind, she didn't have too much time to worry about other things. After writing down a long list of ideas, Barbara and her mother were able to come up with some that would work for their family. For example, if Brad needed urgent attention and Barbara was going someplace with friends, Mom or Barb would call a baby-sitter for Carrie. Because lack of money was a problem in the family, Barbara was willing to split the cost of a baby-sitter with her mom. Barb felt that this was a reasonable compromise.

Barbara was relieved that she and her mom worked this out. She had been afraid to ask her mom for help. Part of her fear came from feeling she had no right to ask for something when Mom had such a big problem as Brad's illness. Barbara was falling into the trap of being a "martyr." She thought she had to give up all of her own desires because of the burdens on Mom. At the same time she was afraid of her own anger. If she did ask Mom to help work out a solution to her problem and Mom said no, what would Barb do then? She might go into a rage and lose control of herself completely.

Learning to Be Assertive

One skill that has helped people like Barbara find ways to meet their own needs, without taking unfair advantage of other people, is assertiveness. About fifteen years ago, this became a popular topic for books, speeches, and talk shows. This approach is just as valuable now as when it first appeared. Since whole books have been written on assertiveness, the subject can't be covered in this chapter. I will give you some of the basic ideas, though.

155

The most important step, I feel, in learning to be assertive is realizing that all of us have rights. That includes the right to have and express our feelings and opinions. At the same time, other people have the right to their own feelings and opinions, which may be different from ours. Learning to be assertive can give you the ability to express your feelings and opinions without ignoring or trampling on the other person's rights, including his right to say no.

Luckily, Barbara's best friend was able to help her see that she wasn't asking her mother for something outrageous. What's more, she was only asking for something, not demanding or threatening. She also wasn't making her mom feel like a terrible mother, or someone who was causing Barbara's problems. Barbara was able to put her feelings into words that still respected her mother's rights. This helped Barbara's mother really hear Barb's side of the problem and feel that her daughter was open to compromise.

Can you think of some feelings and opinions that have been building up inside of you? Have they been making you crabby? Depressed? A good starting point is to list the difficult situations that come up most often and how you feel at those times.

After you've listed them, decide if there's some person who can do something to help. If there is someone with the power to help you, then the next thing to do is to list your rights and the other person's rights. Do you have certain rights in the situation, like the right to have fun sometimes, to have some privacy, or to make certain decisions? Does the other person have rights, like the right to get some help from you sometimes, to be told the truth, and to be able to say no? You may find that it's a lot easier to think of your own rights than to think of the other person's. Yet most people will listen a lot more carefully to what you have to say when you show that you respect their rights and not just your own.

Once you have a clear idea in your mind of each person's rights, then you can put together your assertive statement. Carla, whose sister, Mary, had schizophrenia, was upset that their cousin Tanya never asked about Mary. After thinking it over, Carla decided to say something the next time Tanya called. Her statement went like this: "When you call me on the phone and *never ask about how my sister is doing,* it makes me *think you don't care* about her at all. Then I *feel sad. I would like it if you asked about her* sometimes." The italicized parts are the key ingredients of an assertive statement. They tell *what* the other person is doing, *how* his or her actions *affect* you, how you *feel,* and what *you would like* the person to do. (On the other hand, they don't include telling the other person that she's a worthless creep, which would ignore her right to be treated politely.) It turned out that Tanya didn't ask about Mary because she was afraid Carla would be embarrassed and because she didn't know what to say. When she knew how Carla felt, she was able to act differently.

This "formula" can be used in just about any situation when you have feelings that need to be expressed in words. The key thing for you to remember is that you might not get what you want. The person may not agree with you, and if that person is an adult, he or she may have the power to turn down your request. If that's true, then you might be wondering, "Why bother?" That's a good question.

First of all, if you don't try being assertive about your feelings, you'll never know if it would have worked or not. Second, just saying what you're feeling can help you feel better than holding it inside. Third, there are other people in the world who will listen to you sometimes, and this can be good practice for future situations.

Keep in mind that learning to be assertive takes time and practice. Also, being assertive often seems hardest when you care a lot about the other person and what he or she thinks of you. It can help to start out with little things that don't get you very upset.

158

You can write out what you'll say before you say it, and you can practice in the mirror. If you'll be talking on the phone, you can even have the paper in front of you. Or you can send a short note to the person. If it doesn't work the first time, keep trying! You might even be able to find an assertiveness training class offered through a community recreation program or from a mental health center.

Finding Other Solutions

Barbara and Carla successfully asked someone other than their mentally ill family member to change the behavior that was bothering them. You will probably find that sometimes it is the mentally ill person's actions you want to change. They may be unpredictable, strange, annoying, and embarrassing. They can also be dangerous, and they're certainly difficult to ignore.

You may realize that telling the person how you feel won't improve the situation. For example, if your grandfather has Alzheimer's disease and puts your things where you can't find them, telling him not to probably won't help. In some cases common-sense changes might have to take place. For example, you may need to make an effort not to leave anything where he can get hold of it. Perhaps you'll need a lock on your bedroom door. Other people in the family are likely to have similar problems. Working together to write down as many ideas as you can might help you discover a solution.

There may be times when you'll need the help of people outside your family. If your father becomes violent occasionally, you may need to have the phone numbers of police or emergency rooms handy. It's important to recognize when you can do something about a problem and when you can't. Trying to handle something that's too hard for you might get you or your relative hurt. Keeping a list of agencies that can help is a good idea.

Accepting the Situation

Sometimes the person's symptoms are annoying or embarrassing, but there's nothing you can do. If your mother insists on piling magazines in every room of the house until there's no room to walk, you may not be able to get her to change. Dealing with this type of problem happens in two stages. The first stage boils down to accepting that this is part of your family member's illness. This doesn't mean that it is completely out of her control, but it *is* out of *your* control. If your family member has been in treatment for months or years, or has refused treatment,

160

chances are you're not going to be able to change the person any more than anyone else has. Why get frustrated by trying?

The second stage involves finding ways to let go of your anger, frustration, embarrassment. Then you can go on to better things. Albert Ellis is a well-known therapist who has some good ideas on coping with problems. He has written about the importance of changing your *needs* into *wants*. If you tell yourself, "I need her to stop acting weird," you'll be miserable if she doesn't stop. On the other hand, if you can convince yourself to think, "I want her to stop acting weird, but if she doesn't, I can live with it," you'll be a lot happier.

Relaxation

A good skill that can help you cope with your feelings of frustration is relaxation. Although relaxation is one ingredient in the treatment of anxiety disorders, you don't need to have an anxiety disorder to do it. It can be used by anyone, any time a person feels upset or pressured. It's a way to take care of ourselves and prevent the damage that constant stress can cause.

There are many ways to relax yourself. You can lie in bed or sit in a comfortable chair and just breathe

161

deeply, letting the air out slowly, for a few minutes. A good way to know if you're breathing deeply is to put your hand lightly over your stomach while you breathe. As you breathe in, your stomach should push out, letting the air deep into your lungs. As you breathe out, your stomach will fall gently.

Another way to relax is to close your eyes and concentrate on each part of your body, starting with your feet and slowly moving up to your head. As you think about each part, you can focus on letting the muscles go limp. Some people find it helpful to alternate tensing and relaxing each muscle group to be sure they're really relaxing.

There are tapes and books in libraries and bookstores that have a variety of relaxation instructions in more detail. Like the assertiveness skill, relaxation takes practice. Learning how to calm yourself when things you can't change start getting to you can be a big help.

When Carla's sister, Mary, went into the hospital for the second time, Carla learned relaxation with the psychologist who saw the family for family therapy. Carla had found herself worrying about what would happen to Mary and feeling angry when Mary insisted on believing that certain people were against her. It helped Carla when she learned relax-

162

ation and could then get her mind off Mary. She got good enough at it that she could just take a few deep breaths in order to feel better and in control of herself.

Carla also learned about using imagery. All of us daydream, sometimes without even realizing it. Imagery is a little different from daydreams because you do it on purpose. Picturing yourself lying on a beach, or anywhere else that you consider peaceful, can take you away from your worries, at least temporarily. You can also use imagery to picture yourself in the future, successfully dealing with challenges. When things around you are confusing or upsetting, it helps to remember that you won't be in that situation forever.

Taking Charge of Your Own Life

There are lots of other things you can do to make your own life better. Finding ways to make money— baby-sitting, doing errands for neighbors, helping clean up or serve at parties—can give you the freedom to do more things that you enjoy, or to save for college or your own apartment. When you earn your own money, you won't have to add to the stress in the family by asking for money all the time. Learning new hobbies or getting better at old ones can help you feel good about yourself and get your mind off your problems. Letting out your frustrations by dancing, jogging, or another physical activity can also help cut down on your stress level.

Two Things to Remember

There are two important ideas I'd like to leave you with. One is the "Serenity Prayer," used in Alcoholics Anonymous. Regardless of our religious beliefs, it's something that all of us can benefit from. It goes: "God grant me the serenity to accept the things I can't change, the courage to change the things I can, and the wisdom to know the difference between the two." Think about it. How much frustration and guilt will you avoid if you can accept that your relative has an illness that may not get better? And that some people may continue to disappoint you even when you talk to them about it? And that you can accomplish at least some of the things you want to? Probably a lot.

The other idea comes from an essay by a writer named Sydney Harris. I read it about ten years ago and it has stuck in my mind ever since. The essay told of two men who walked up to a newsstand. The

164

first man put down his money and picked up a paper. He greeted the "newsie" selling the papers but got a gruff reply. He thanked the man and continued walking with his friend. His friend asked why he was polite to the newsie after being treated so rudely. The rest of the essay contained the first man's explanation.

The main point of the essay was that all of us have the choice of acting or reacting. When we *act,* we do what we feel is right. When we *react,* we let someone else's mood or behavior determine how we feel and behave. When we are able to *act,* our lives can go more smoothly. We don't have to wait for someone to compliment us before we can feel good about ourselves. We also don't have to stumble into depression when someone else doesn't like our looks, clothing, opinions, or actions.

How many times have you let yourself be dragged down by someone else's bad mood? Or swept up by someone's good mood? Of course, there are times when someone else's behavior can affect you. A teacher's bad mood might lead to extra homework for the whole class. Or your mentally ill relative may decide not to tell you about an important phone call you got while you were out. That's different. That can call for assertiveness or some creative problem

165

solving. But aren't there times when you've done something, not because you felt it was right, but because of what someone else was doing?

Suppose you've been doing homework, and it's close to the time your mom will be home from her job. You're thinking that you'll vacuum the living room as soon as your math problems are done. Then your mom comes home a few minutes early with a headache and hollers, "I thought I told you to vacuum the living room today!" You can react to her anger and say, "I was going to, till you got home in such a crabby mood—now I won't!" Or you can act and say, "I'm planning to do it as soon as my math is done. I realize you probably had a rough day, but I would appreciate it if you didn't take it out on me." Which response seems easier? Which will be more helpful to you in the long run?

I'm certain no one always acts calmly and confidently, ignoring the comments of other people. Still, you can save yourself a lot of upset by keeping in mind that you don't *have* to let other people's annoying behavior affect you—especially with a mentally ill family member in the house. You need to remind yourself of the things you can't change about that person. Then you can decide what your goal is—how you want to act toward that person— and try each day to achieve it.

166

It Helps to Get Some Help

It's important to realize that the ideas I've talked about aren't easy. They may be too hard for you to try on your own. Talking to a school counselor or a mental health professional may be necessary. If you're already in family therapy, you might ask the therapist for a few individual sessions if your family can handle the cost. If there's a university nearby, there may be a psychological clinic where you can go for a very small fee. By talking to your parents or another adult you trust, you can find out how to get this help. The main thing is, do it! No matter how scary or impossible it seems, make yourself do it, or get a friend to give you moral support and encouragement. The first step is always the hardest!

11

◆

Helping Your Family

In the last chapter I talked about some ways you can help yourself cope with the difficulties of having a mentally ill family member. There's an important reason why that topic was placed before the topic of this chapter, helping your family. It's hard, if not impossible, to help other people while you're focused on your own hurt. Looking outside of yourself to what other people are dealing with is a luxury that comes with having a certain amount of confidence and peace of mind. If you've been working on making your own life better, and you're starting to make some progress, you may be ready at least to think about helping your family get along better.

Everyone Is Affected

I've already pointed out many of the problems your relative's mental illness might be causing for you. It's no surprise, then, that others in your family are affected in similar ways. Depending on each person's role in the family, he or she may also have some reactions that are different from yours. Since you're all in this situation together, it makes sense to try to help one another get through it. Somehow troubles don't seem quite as bad when you're not trying to solve them alone.

A good place to start is with another list. Write down each person's name, and next to it write how that person is affected by the fact of mental illness in your family. Is she frightened by the ill person's strange behavior? Younger brothers and sisters might find it even more upsetting than you do. Is he stressed by worries about how to pay for the treatment? Your parents, especially, may feel overwhelmed by the cost of the illness. Is she sad that her marriage is being hurt by the illness? Is he angry that the treatment isn't working as well as he had hoped? Put yourself in each person's place for a moment. You can probably think of even more ways that the mental illness is affecting the other mem-

169

bers of your family. Don't forget to put your own concerns on the list, too.

Helping Others Can Help You

Now that you have this list, remind yourself that it's not your job to solve all those problems. Simply being aware of what each person is going through can help you and your family. Suppose your little brother is angry that your depressed father never plays with him. Maybe talking with your brother about your own frustration with Dad's illness will let him know he's not alone. It may help him talk about what's going on in his mind. Perhaps you can make plans with him to go to a baseball game or take a hike in the woods. You can be an important role model, showing your younger brothers or sisters how to find substitutes for what they want but can't have.

By paying attention to what other people in the family are feeling, you can avoid making them feel worse and even help them feel a little better. The result can make your life easier, too. Suppose your mom is tired every night after working overtime, trying to make enough money for your father's treatment. You and other family members can help by taking turns preparing supper. Mom might then

170

have more time and energy to take you to the library or band practice. She might even see that you're getting more grown up and decide you're ready for more privileges. Your dad would still be ill, but he would be even if the rest of you didn't help one another. Seeing your own life change in a positive direction can make his illness a bit easier for you to take.

When Allison's mother was still in therapy for her agoraphobia, Allison organized a neighborhood play camp for five children that summer. She asked her mother to be the camp lunch maker, which boosted her mother's growing self-confidence. Allison had Ben and Joey help her plan games and craft activities. Not only did it keep her brothers busy, but Allison made some money. She also learned about keeping children active and happy. She was then able to write about her experiences on her applications for a real camp job the next year.

Keep Communicating

Some families find it helpful to have a family meeting every week or so. Since school, work, and activities can make life hectic, there may be few chances for everyone to sit down together. You may need to put the meeting on the calendar, with every-

171

one's understanding that they shouldn't make other plans for that time. People can take turns being "timekeeper" each week, making sure each person has a certain number of minutes to talk about what he or she needs or would like. If people have learned how to use the assertiveness skill I described in chapter 10, they can really listen to each other without trying to shift blame or change the subject. The family "secretary" for the week can write down any decisions that are made, so they can be reviewed at the next meeting to see how they worked out.

After Kyle's accident, when he seemed to be having trouble getting back to being his old self, his brother Dwayne was upset. Kyle wasn't paying attention to him, and his mom was busy working and trying to get Kyle to his therapy sessions without missing too much work. It seemed as if his family had fallen apart. When Dwayne finally told his mom how he felt, they worked out a system of leaving messages for each other. Either could ask for a meeting if there was a need to talk about something. Using this system, Dwayne's mom asked him to help choose a time when they could go shopping together for his school supplies. She also let Dwayne know that when he needed to go somewhere and she couldn't take him, she'd try to arrange for someone else to do it. When Dwayne had no one to take him to a big basketball game, his mom was able to have his uncle and cousins take him.

An important part of becoming assertive involves listening to the other person. Many of us have learned over the years to tune out when someone tells us what we don't want to hear. "Your grades need to improve." "You forgot to take out the garbage." "Where's the bread I asked you to get at the store?" It helps when we start believing, however, that we have rights, including the right to make mistakes, and that other people have a right to their opinions. Then it's a lot easier to hear someone's complaints without feeling attacked. When Dwayne told his mother that he felt sad because Kyle was ignoring him and she was so busy, his mother realized it had been a while since she and Dwayne had spent any time together. Instead of blaming Kyle for her busy schedule, she told Dwayne she could understand how he felt. She didn't assume that he was telling her she was the worst mother in the world and that she had to defend herself. She accepted the fact that she might have been forgetting about Dwayne's needs. If Dwayne had told her, "You're a rotten mother," she might not have paid attention to what was really bugging him.

173

We All Need to Hear Kind Words

As much as we don't like hearing complaints, we usually like getting compliments. We've all felt that special pride when someone, whether it's a parent, a teacher, or a work supervisor, let us know we were doing a good job. Yet what about the other person? He or she likes compliments as much as we do. How many times do we remember to tell a teacher, "That was an interesting class today," or say to a parent, "It was really nice of you to let me out of doing the dishes so I could go to the movie with my friends"? It seems to be human nature to notice when people irritate us but to forget to comment when they make life more pleasant. Suppose you start trying to compliment every person in your family once each day. You may find them doing the same thing back to you after a while. If not, you can assertively remind them, "When you tell me that I've done something you like, I feel good. Could you try to do it more often?"

Agreeing to Disagree

In spite of your efforts to help and understand the other people in your family, you may still find that you just don't like how they're reacting to your men-

174

tally ill family member. In that case you may simply have to accept what you can't change. Everyone has a different timetable for coping with problems. The other person may never react the way you'd like him or her to.

Nevertheless, it's important for you and your family to plan times together when you can just forget about mental illness for a few hours. If you build up a reserve of good feelings in other areas of your life, the disagreements and disappointments won't destroy your relationships. Mary's sister, Carla, never understood how her father could continue to get angry with Mary for the odd or irresponsible things she did or said. In spite of this, Carla and her mother would arrange picnics, vacations, and other enjoyable times with her dad, when they all agreed not to discuss Mary's illness. That way, when she needed help with college applications, Carla and her dad worked on them together, having kept their relationship going even though they had different responses to Mary.

The main tools you have for working on better family relationships are communicating your feelings, trying to understand how other people are feeling, and doing what is within your power to make things better. In fact, helping yourself and helping your family aren't all that different.

175

Conclusion

In the preceding chapters, I've led you through the maze of mental illness as we now understand it. Research continues into the reasons why these disorders develop and what can be done about them. New discoveries are happening all the time, offering hope to families like yours.

I've also given you suggestions to help you cope with your relative's mental illness. The suggestions won't change the fact that this person is ill, or the fact that you're concerned about this person and the impact of his or her illness on you and your family. The only things that you can change are within you—your attitude toward the person, your understanding of the illness, and your ability to focus on making your own life better.

You may forget at times that you have your own

combination of talents. Your skills may lie in traditional areas such as school or sports, or in a more unusual direction, like making people laugh. If you haven't discovered your talents yet, don't worry. We keep learning and developing as we get older, even after our school days are over.

You also have a set of interests that are particular to you—the things that grab your attention in a room full of competing activities. Your interests and talents may be similar, since we all enjoy doing things we're good at. Or you may enjoy dabbling in something that's just fun, like cooking or playing drums, even if the results aren't good enough, in your view, to show everyone.

And let's not forget about needs and wishes. You may feel most comfortable when you're with one or two close friends, or you may love having the attention of a large group of people. Perhaps you dream of opening your own restaurant some day, or you want to be the first woman president.

All of these parts of you are important. They make you different from anyone else, and they give you a blueprint for your future life, even if it changes from time to time. Your best bet is to work on channeling these talents, interests, and needs into hobbies, relationships, and a job or career you can enjoy. In that way, you'll have the satisfaction of feeling good about what you're doing, a lot of the time anyway. It's true that, even if you do this, you'll still have mental illness in your family. But your life will also have its bright side, and the results will be worth the effort.

Appendix
Finding a Support Group
for You and Your Family

Support groups have been helpful to families of the mentally ill. Sharing problems and ideas with people who are going through the same thing can really lighten the burden of dealing with a difficult situation. Many support organizations are available, some nationally and others in limited areas. Each group has different activities, which range from giving emotional support to providing education about the disorder and new findings. Some even encourage members to become politically involved, working to get new laws passed or to increase public awareness of problems that patients and their families face. Only you and your family can decide what type of group might meet your needs and interests.

A good place to start in finding a support group that can help your family is by asking the mental health professional who is working with your relative. Also, the Yellow Pages in your area will have listings under "Mental Health Services" that may be useful. When you find an organization that might be suitable, here are some questions you can ask. The answers will help you decide whether to try it.

1. Is there a membership fee? If so, can you or your family afford it? What services or benefits do you get, and do they seem worth the fee? For example, are there meetings, a newsletter, speakers on important topics?

2. Is the group mainly for people with a particular disorder, for family members, or both? How often does the group meet? Does the group's schedule suit yours? Are people your age involved?

3. Does the group have a particular philosophy or set of goals? Are they compatible with your own? Is the group strongly in favor of or against certain treatment approaches? If you are unsure of how you feel about mental health issues, will the group give you a chance to hear more than one viewpoint?

4. How long has the group in your area been around? Have there been many changes in leader-

ship, meeting schedules, and so on? You may like joining a new group and helping to shape it into what you want. On the other hand, you may feel more comfortable in a group that's well established and not likely to change much.

5. Here are the toughest questions, and they're for you to ask yourself. Are you nervous about joining a group and going to a meeting? Are you afraid because the group doesn't sound right for you or because it's a new experience? If you're hesitant because it's new and different, that's natural. It's easy to make excuses for not going when you're not sure what to expect. Getting a family member or friend to go along can get you over the initial hurdle. You might even find yourself thinking afterward, "How did I ever get along without this?"

If you're unable to find a nearby group of people in a situation similar to yours, the following organizations may be able to help you locate one. Again, getting answers to the questions I've listed will help you decide what's right for you. If all else fails, your family might even consider starting a group. The mental health professionals you've encountered so far could probably help you get started. In any case, good luck in your search!

Be sure to enclose a self-addressed envelope with two first-class stamps on it when you write to any of these organizations.

Alzheimer's Disease and Related Disorders
     Association
70 E. Lake Street
Suite 600
Chicago, IL 60601

American Anorexia/Bulimia Association
133 Cedar Lane
Teaneck, NJ 07666

Anorexia Nervosa and Related Eating Disorders
P.O. Box 5102
Eugene, OR 97405

Depressives Anonymous
329 E. 62nd Street
New York, NY 10021

Emotions Anonymous
P.O. Box 4245
St. Paul, MN 55104

National Alliance for the Mentally Ill
P.O. Box 12827
Arlington, VA 22209

National Anorexic Aid Society
5796 Karl Road
Columbus, OH 43229

National Association of Anorexia Nervosa and
    Associated Disorders
Box 7
Highland Park, IL 60035

National Depressive and Manic-Depressive
    Association
Merchandise Mart
Box 3395
Chicago, IL 60654

Phobia Society of America
133 Rollins Avenue
Suite 4B
Rockville, MD 20852

Glossary

Agoraphobia. Extreme fear and avoidance of public places, especially situations in which escape seems impossible. This usually results in an inability to leave one's home. Panic attacks may also occur.

Alcoholism. A disorder involving long-term, excessive alcohol use, leading to serious problems in the person's life and relationships. Stopping alcohol use is difficult and brings withdrawal symptoms.

Alzheimer's disease. A brain disease that involves a gradual decline in memory, other thinking skills, and self-care ability, as well as personality changes.

Anorexia nervosa. An eating disorder in which fear of being fat, a desire to be perfect, refusal to

185

eat, and excessive exercise are associated with dangerous amounts of weight loss.

Antianxiety medication. Medication used to treat anxiety disorders. There are several different types.

Antidepressant. One of several medications used to treat severe depression.

Antipsychotic medication. One of several medications used to control the delusions and hallucinations of schizophrenia. They also help prevent a relapse of symptoms.

Anxiety. A generalized state of fear or uneasiness, ranging from mild to severe and sometimes occurring without a known cause.

Anxiety disorder. A condition in which intense anxiety hinders a person's ability to carry out normal tasks of living. Specific types include phobias, obsessive-compulsive disorder, and post-traumatic stress disorder.

Art therapy. A type of activities therapy in which painting, sculpting, and other creative activities help people express feelings and gain self-esteem.

Assertiveness. A communication approach that involves honest expression of one's own feelings and respect for the feelings and rights of others. Training programs that teach this skill are widely available.

Binge. An episode of uncontrolled, excessive eating, usually of high-calorie sweets and starchy foods.

Biofeedback. A relaxation training procedure for learning to reduce blood pressure, muscle tension, and other signs of anxiety. Electronic instruments give information about these internal responses, helping the person learn how to change them.

Bipolar disorder. A serious mood disorder in which depressive and manic episodes occur. The length of time between mood shifts can range from days to months.

Bulimarexia. A word sometimes used to describe an eating disorder that combines features of anorexia nervosa and bulimia.

Bulimia. An eating disorder consisting of compulsive, uncontrolled eating episodes, usually followed by voluntary vomiting and/or laxative and diuretic use.

CAT scan. An X-ray technique that takes pictures from many angles in order to help detect physi-

cal problems such as the brain changes associated with Alzheimer's disease.
Clinical psychologist. A person with a doctoral degree, or less often a master's degree, in psychology, who is trained in diagnosis and
treatment of mental disorders.
Cognitive therapy. A type of treatment for depression
that helps people use new ways of thinking to
achieve changes in their emotions and behavior.
Commitment. A decision by a judge or other au-
thority that a person is to be hospitalized for
mental illness without his consent. Laws vary
from state to state on how this is done. Usually
the person must be shown to be an immediate
danger to himself or others.
Community Mental Health Centers (CMHC's).
Clinics set up in accordance with federal law as
an alternative to private mental health treatment. Each one serves a certain geographic
area and charges fees according to each person's ability to pay.

Day treatment. Programs for treating people who
need intensive psychological or psychiatric care
but are able to live outside a hospital. Patients
attend various therapies during the day and return to their homes at night.

188

Dehydration. Abnormal depletion of body fluids, a life-threatening condition that can result from abuse of laxatives or diuretics.

Deinstitutionalization. A practice in treatment of mental illness in which patients are released from mental hospitals, or psychiatric units of general hospitals, as quickly as possible and are then treated on an outpatient basis. They may live with their families, in halfway houses, or alone. This approach has resulted in the closing of many mental hospitals.

Delusion. A false belief that is held in spite of conflicting evidence and in spite of what most people believe.

Dementia. A decline or defect in thinking ability, especially memory, caused by Alzheimer's disease or other brain conditions. It can be temporary or permanent.

Depression (major). A mood disorder in which sadness, apathy, and hopelessness persist and prevent normal daily activities.

Diuretic. A medication that increases voiding of urine and is used by some people with eating disorders to aid in weight loss.

Eating disorder. A serious disturbance in eating, which can include excessive, uncontrolled food intake, severely limited food intake, or a combination of both.

Electroconvulsive therapy (ECT). A type of treatment for severe mental illness, usually depression, in which electric current is used to bring on a seizure.

Family therapy. A type of psychotherapy focusing on interactions and relationships among family members, rather than the feelings and behavior of one member who is identified as the patient.

Fight or flight. A set of physical reactions to danger that prepares a person to confront the threat or escape from it. Reactions include rapid heart rate, sweating, chest pains, rapid breathing, and feelings of fear.

Group therapy. One of several psychotherapy approaches in which one or two therapists work with several patients at a time.

Halfway house. A special residence with programs to help formerly hospitalized mental patients readjust to living in the community.

Hallucinations. Sensations that have no basis in reality. A person may see things or hear voices that are not there. False sensations of touch, taste, smell, and internal bodily feelings may also occur.

Hypomanic. Having a mood of abnormally high spirits and excitement that is less intense than mania.

Imagery. Mental pictures of situations and activities, used to help a person relax or cope with a difficult situation.

Interpersonal therapy. A type of psychotherapy for depression that focuses on improving present relationships.

Lithium. A type of mineral salt that is used to treat and prevent recurrences of bipolar disorder.

Mania. A state of extreme excitement involving poor judgment, rapidly changing ideas, restlessness, and unrealistic plans. This is one phase of bipolar disorder.

Manic-depressive illness. A term sometimes used to refer to bipolar disorder.

Mental illness. A serious disturbance of thought,

emotions, and/or behavior that disrupts a person's ability to get along with other people and meet the demands of daily life without treatment.

Mood disorder. A mental illness consisting of a major disturbance of moods. This category includes bipolar disorder and major depression.

Music therapy. Programs using dance, singing, and musical instruments to help people express their feelings, increase control over their behavior, and gain self-esteem.

Neuroleptic. A drug that affects thinking and or emotions, also called antipsychotic.

Obsessive-compulsive disorder. An anxiety disorder consisting of repetitive, unwanted ideas (obsessions) and/or urges (compulsions) to perform certain actions.

Padded cell. A small room with cushioned walls where an out-of-control patient could be kept to prevent him from harming himself.

Panic attack. A sudden and upsetting state of intense anxiety that includes an overwhelming desire to escape from the situation and strong physical responses such as rapid heart rate and breathing.

Phobia. A strong and persistent fear of an object or situation, resulting in avoidance of the object or situation. The fear is more extreme than the situation calls for and usually interferes with some aspect of the person's life.

Phobia clinics. Treatment centers with specialized programs for helping people with phobias and their families.

Postpartum depression. A reaction of depressed mood that occurs in some women following childbirth. The severity can range from mild "blues," which go away without treatment, to, less commonly, major depression.

Post-traumatic stress disorder (PTSD). A group of symptoms that occurs sometime after an extremely upsetting experience, such as combat. It can show up months or years after the event. Anxiety, sleep problems, withdrawal from other people, lack of feelings, and brief episodes of reliving the event can occur.

Psychiatric nurse. Someone with a nursing education who specializes in the care and treatment of mental patients.

Psychiatric social worker. Someone with a master's

degree, or sometimes a doctoral degree, in social work, who specializes in doing psychotherapy with people who have mental and emotional problems.

Psychiatrist. A medical doctor specializing in diagnosis and treatment of mental illness.

Psychosis. A condition in which a person is out of touch with reality. "Psychotic" may describe someone with schizophrenia, severe depression, or severe mania.

Psychotherapy. Any of a variety of treatments for emotional and behavior disorders in which a therapist talks with someone about problems, feelings, relationships, and how to improve or deal with these.

Purge. An aspect of bulimia in which the person tries to avoid gaining weight from bingeing by voluntarily vomiting or misusing laxatives and diuretics.

Reality orientation. A program used in some nursing homes to help Alzheimer's disease patients focus on facts of present, daily life, such as who they are and where they are.

Recreational therapy. Programs that involve people in group activities to help improve their

social skills and reduce their isolation and a-
pathy.

Relaxation training. A series of breathing and muscle exercises that lead to deep feelings of physical and mental relaxation. It is often used as
part of a treatment program for anxiety disorders.

Residual schizophrenia. The phase of schizophrenia
when psychotic, bizarre symptoms are gone,
but problems in relating to others, thinking
logically, and experiencing emotions persist.

Sandwich generation. A term used to describe middle-aged adults caught between responsibilities
to their children, who are not yet independent,
and to their parents, who are becoming less
able to take care of themselves.

Schizophrenia. A major mental illness or group of
illnesses. Symptoms can include disturbed
thinking, confusion about one's own identity,
lack of interest in one's surroundings, hallucinations, and lack of feelings, or feelings that are
inappropriate to the situation.

Shock treatments. *See* Electroconvulsive therapy.

Straitjacket. A garment that used to be put on mental patients whose behavior could not be con-

trolled. Long sleeves wrapped around the patient's body to prevent the person from injuring himself or others.

Stress. A situation in which the environment makes greater demands on a person than he or she can handle. The word also refers sometimes to the body's emergency responses to unusual demands on the person.

Stressor. An intense or severe event that has a negative impact on a person.

Suicide. Taking of one's life voluntarily, usually as a result of hopelessness that conditions will improve. It is a danger whenever someone is depressed.

Support group. An organization consisting of people who share a common problem and who try to help each other by providing encouragement and understanding. An educational aspect may involve guest speakers or other methods for learning new information about the problem. An advocacy aspect may involve efforts to get new laws passed or to help the public understand the problems better.

Tardive dyskinesia. A side effect of long-term use of antipsychotic medications that involves lip smacking and other involuntary movements.

Early detection and stopping the medication, or reducing the dosage, can eliminate the symptoms.

Trauma, emotional. An intensely upsetting event that can have long-lasting effects on a person's well-being.

References

American Psychiatric Association. 1987. *Diagnostic and Statistical Manual of Mental Disorders* (Third Edition—Revised). Washington, D.C.

Bernheim, K., Lewine, R. R. J., and Beale, C. T. 1982. *The Caring Family.* New York: Random House.

Burns, D. D. 1980. *Feeling Good: The New Mood Therapy.* New York: Signet.

Christenson, H., Hadzi-Pavlovic, D., Andrews, G., and Mattick, R. 1987. Behavior therapy and tricyclic medication in the treatment of obsessive-compulsive disorder: A quantitative review. *Journal of Consulting and Clinical Psychology* 55: 701–11.

Cohen, D., and Eisdorfer, C. 1986. *The Loss of Self.* New York: W. W. Norton & Co.

Coyne, J. C., Kessler, R. C., Tal, M., Turnbull, J.,

Wortman, C. B., and Greden, J. F. 1987. Living with a depressed person. *Journal of Consulting and Clinical Psychology* 55: 347–52.

Donlon, P. T., Schaffer, C. B., Ericksen, S. E., Pepitone-Arreola-Rockwell, F., and Schaffer, L. C. 1983. *A Manual of Psychotropic Drugs.* Bowie, MD: Robert J. Brady Co.

Ellis, A., and Harper, R. A. 1979. *New Guide to Rational Living.* N. Hollywood, CA: Wilshire Publishing Co.

Ericksen, C. 1986. *Depression Is Curable.* Clackamas, OR: Rainbow Press.

Families of the Mentally Ill Collective. 1986. *Families Helping Families—Living with Schizophrenia.* New York: W. W. Norton & Co.

Frank, J. 1985. *Alzheimer's Disease: The Silent Epidemic.* Minneapolis: Lerner Publications.

Gold, M. S., with Morris, L. B. 1987. *The Good News About Depression.* New York: Villard Books.

Goldman, P., and Fuller, T. 1983. *Charlie Company.* New York: William Morrow & Co.

Goldstein, A. 1987. *Overcoming Agoraphobia.* New York: Viking Penguin.

Group for the Advancement of Psychiatry. 1986. *A Family Affair.* New York: Brunner/Mazel.

Harris, S. J. "Act vs. React." (Date, place unknown.)

Hendin, H., and Haas, A. P. 1984. *Wounds of War.* New York: Basic Books.

Kaplan, A. S., and Woodside, D. B. 1987. Biological aspects of anorexia nervosa and bulimia nervosa. *Journal of Consulting and Clinical Psychology* 55: 645–53.

Krantz, S. E., and Moos, R. H. 1987. Functioning and life context among spouses of remitted and nonremitted depressed patients. *Journal of Consulting and Clinical Psychology* 55: 353–60.

Langone, J. 1985. The war that has no ending. *Discover* (June): 44–54.

Mitchell, J. E., and Eckert, E. 1987. Scope and significance of eating disorders. *Journal of Consulting and Clinical Psychology* 55: 628–34.

Niebuhr, R. Serenity Prayer. In Bingham, J. 1961. *Courage to Change.* New York: Charles Scribner's Sons.

O'Neill, C. B. 1982. *Starving for Attention.* New York: Continuum Publishing Co.

Papolos, D. F., and Papolos, J. 1987. *Overcoming Depression.* New York: Harper & Row.

Polivy, J., and Herman, C. P. 1987. Diagnosis and treatment of normal eating. *Journal of Consulting and Clinical Psychology* 55: 635–44.

Powell, L. S., and Courtice, K. 1983. *Alzheimer's Dis-*

ease. Reading, MA: Addison-Wesley Publishing Co.

Strober, M., and Humphrey, L. L. 1987. Familial contributions to the etiology and course of anorexia nervosa and bulimia. *Journal of Consulting and Clinical Psychology* 55: 654–59.

Thompson, E. H., Jr., and Doll, W. 1982. The burden of families coping with the mentally ill: An invisible crisis. *Family Relations* 31: 379–88.

Torrey, E. F. 1983. *Surviving Schizophrenia: A Family Manual.* New York: Harper & Row.

United States Department of Health and Human Services. September 1984. *Alzheimer's Disease.* Report of the Secretary's Task Force on Alzheimer's Disease.

Van der Kolk, B. 1987. *Psychological Trauma.* Washington, D.C.: American Psychiatric Press.

Van Devanter, L., with Morgan, C. 1983. *Home Before Morning.* New York: Beaufort Books.

Vine, P. 1982. *Families in Pain.* New York: Pantheon Books.

Vonnegut, M. 1975. *The Eden Express.* New York: Praeger Publishers.

Walsh, M. 1985. *Schiz-o-phre-nia.* New York: Warner Books.

Wilson, R. R. 1986. *Don't Panic.* New York: Harper & Row.

Index

Harris, Sydney J., 164
helping family members
get along better
through acceptance of
disagreements,
174–75
through assertive
communication, 172
through awareness of
others' reactions,
169–70
through family
meetings, 171–72
through listening, 172
through praise, 174
Home Before Morning
(Van Devanter),
94–95
hospital treatment
of eating disorders,
137–38
of obsessive-
compulsive
disorder, 88
psychologists' role in,
149
psychiatrists' role in,
149
of schizophrenia, 38–
41, 47–48, 49, 50
hypomanic symptoms,
59

imagery, 163
interpersonal therapy,
66

lithium, 68–69

mania, 61
manic-depressive illness,
8
See also bipolar disorder
medication
antianxiety, 88–89, 94
antidepressant, 63,
88–89, 138
antipsychotic, 41–43
for eating disorders,
138
finding the right dose
of, 41, 42, 63,
64–65
for mood disorders
bipolar disorder,
68–69
depression, 63–65
for post-traumatic
stress disorder, 105
for schizophrenia,
41–43
side effects of
appearing as
Alzheimer's
symptoms, 111